A *Vade Mecum* for Medical Students and Residents

OSLER FOR

WHITE COAT

POCKETS

by
Joseph B. VanderVeer, Jr., M.D.
and
Charles S. Bryan, M.D.

AMERICAN OSLER SOCIETY

© 2017

Osler for White Coat Pockets
A *Vade Mecum*

Library of Congress Number: 2017901031

International Standard Book Number: 978-1-60126-524-1

Printed at
Masthof Press
219 Mill Road | Morgantown, PA 19543-9516
www.Masthof.com

CONTENTS

PATIENT AND PHYSICIAN

THE TRAINING YEARS

FOUR APPENDICES

PREFACE

A basic issue for contemporary American society is how to bring the technological and humanistic features of medicine into balance.

— Stanley Joel Reiser[1]

I always thought being compassionate and respectful would be the easy part of being a doctor and gaining the large amount of knowledge would be the hard part. I have realized it is the exact opposite.

— Remark of a third-year medical student

This small pocket book (called a *Vade Mecum* from the Latin, meaning *Go with Me*) has been written for medical students and residents in the belief that the counsel of William Osler has much to offer them. The authors are members of the American Osler Society (AOS), a group of physicians, historians and librarians who seek to promulgate the ideals and values of Sir William Osler. (His biographical sketch is found in Appendix A and the Society is described in Appendix B.)

Almost fifty years ago, Drs. John P. McGovern and H. Grant Taylor, attending the annual meeting of the Association of American Medical Colleges (AAMC), heard medical students express dissatisfaction with their education which they frequently

---

[1] Reiser (2009), 188.

described as "dehumanizing." The students, they concluded, seemed to be expressing needs that Sir William Osler (1849-1919) addressed during his lifetime. He was the most celebrated physician in the English-speaking world at the turn of the twentieth century. Two years later, McGovern and Taylor helped organize a symposium to mark the 50th anniversary of the death of Osler, which was published under the title *Humanism in Medicine*.[2] It was the last major gathering of people who had known Osler personally.

McGovern[3] became the driving force behind the founding of the AOS in 1970, which evolved into an international organization to perpetuate Osler's life and ideals. One author of this *Vade Mecum*, surgeon Joe VanderVeer, Jr., taught at the University of Oregon in Portland, OR, and at the University of Arizona in Phoenix. Author Charles S. Bryan, an internist specializing in infectious disease, was professor of medicine at the University of South Carolina. We share our experience jointly throughout the book.

Osler once said he'd like his epitaph to be "I taught students in the wards," and indeed, his forte was bedside teaching. Nowadays one rarely encounters bedside teaching, and much has changed since Osler's day. But we believe his ideals and aphorisms are still inspiring, for he was the epitome of the humanist physician. They form the basis for this manual, in which we share many of his counsels as well as some of our own. It is meant to supplement efforts now being explored by medical educators and by outside organizations, notably the Arnold P. Gold Foundation,[4] to

---

[2] McGovern and Burns (1973).

[3] Boutwell (2014).

[4] Arnold P. Gold Foundation (2016) see http://www.gold-foundation.org/about-us/faqs/

promote humanism in medical practice. We believe that the character of the physician still matters in an age during which health care is increasingly seen as a commodity to be bought and sold like any other. Several of our chapters discuss character and virtue ethics.

Efforts to encapsulate the best of Osler's wisdom and aphoristic advice began with Osler himself, who in 1904 published *Aequanimitas With Other Addresses to Medical Students, Nurses and Practitioners of Medicine,* a book that consisted of 18 addresses delivered between 1899 and 1903, *Aequanimitas* solidified Osler's reputation as an inspirational figure for physicians, just as his 1892 textbook *The Principles and Practice of Medicine* had established his reputation as the foremost generalist-physician in the English-speaking world. We cite many of Osler's writings in this book (most are in bold-face type), and for simplicity in the footnotes, his essays and addresses found in *Aequanimitas* are named by title only, with complete information given in the bibliography. Other referenced authors are cited in footnotes by name and year of their publication, with the complete citation given in the bibliography. That extensive list of references also includes a number of other collections of Osler's essays and addresses[5] published after *Aequanimitas* was brought out.

In the text that follows, there are many mentions made to religion, especially Christianity, as a means to explain moral or ethical principles. It is not our intention to alienate persons of other systems of belief, but instead to use these references to help our readers glean insight that will help them become more competent and caring physicians.

---

[5] These include Bean (1950); Keynes (1951); Verney (1957); Roland (1982); Bryan (1997); Silverman et al (2008).

We recognize all too well that today's students and residents, immersed as they are in digital technology, may lack the time and inclination to delve into the humanities to the extent that members of previous generations of physicians were encouraged to do. Perhaps this small volume, kept in white coat pockets as a *Vade Mecum,* will be of help, and we hope to receive feedback and comments from our readers. We hope each of you will be motivated to put together a bedside library of your own. (See Appendix C.)

"The authors will thankfully receive any communication that can tend to render this book more perfect and in case [the profession] ever calls for a second edition, such new facts or observations as occur shall be inserted with suitable acknowledgements."[6]

Joseph B. VanderVeer, Jr., M.D.
Devon, Pennsylvania
(He is JBV in text vignettes)
joebvv2@live.com

Charles S. Bryan, M.D.
Columbia, South Carolina
(He is CSB in text vignettes)
cboslerian@gmail.com

---

[6] This quotation is a transcription from the preface of the first edition of William Withering's *An Account of the Foxglove,* 1785.

ACKNOWLEDGEMENTS

The authors are grateful for the assistance of several persons whose review and critiques were helpful in preparing this volume, including Drs. Herbert Swick, Richard Colgan, Tyler Hughes, Mary McGrath, Russ Kerbel, Jack Coulehan, Darrell Kirch, and medical students Michael John Sylvester and Timothy Smile. The financial support of the John P. McGovern Foundation is gratefully acknowledged.

THE TRADITIONS OF MEDICINE

THE QUEST

I n his foreword to the 2015 *New York Times Book of Medicine* physician-writer Abraham Verghese wrote:

> The AIDS epidemic changed my career and my life. Among the many things I learned was that when one could not cure, one could *heal*. By that I mean that even in this fatal illness, one could help the patient and the family come to terms with the disease, one could relieve pain and suffering; I learned that healing occurred by one's presence, by caring, by being there for the patient through thick and thin. It was something the horse-and-buggy doctor of a century before understood; even in those pre-antibiotic and pre-vaccine days when scarlet fever and typhoid and tuberculosis were untreatable scourges, the doctor still had much to offer.[1]

The physician of today has a great deal more to offer than in the pre-antibiotic and pre-vaccine days. Osler's era was like

---

[1] Verghese, introduction to Kolata (2015).

that, but the humanistic spirit that motivated Osler still is relevant today. New diseases like AIDS or SARS or Ebola bring new challenges, but beyond the technology and the new therapeutic agents, the relationship of patient to physician remains as the basis for healing. As students and residents aspiring to become outstanding physicians, you are on a Quest for wisdom, knowledge, and skills that will make you extraordinary doctors.

In an 1892 address at the University of Minnesota, Osler congratulated the students on choosing medicine as a career:

> **Students of Medicine, Apprentices of the Guild, with whom are the promises, and in whom [we center] our hopes—let me congratulate you on the choice of calling which offers a combination of intellectual and moral interests found in no other profession, and are not met with at all in the common pursuits of life—a combination which, in the words of Sir James Paget, "offers the most complete and constant union of those three qualities which have the greatest charm for pure and active minds—novelty, utility, and charity."[2]**

Indeed, **novelty**, **utility** and **charity** are three important facets of the challenge of medicine, of the Quest that you have embarked upon. CSB experienced that challenge in mid-career much as Dr. Abraham Verghese did.[3] The **novelty** was facing a totally new and frightening disease; **utility** was involved in seeking a treatment, hopefully a cure for the disease, once it had been identified; and **charity** was to characterize the care given to his patients. Here is what occurred.

---

[2] Teacher and student.
[3] Bryan (2003).

As an infectious disease specialist, the HIV/AIDS epidemic gave me the opportunity to live through what amounted to a truncated history of medicine between 1981, when "AIDS" first came to the world's attention, and 1996, when highly active antiretroviral therapy (HAART) became widely available. In retrospect, it was an attenuated, emotional roller coaster as shown below.

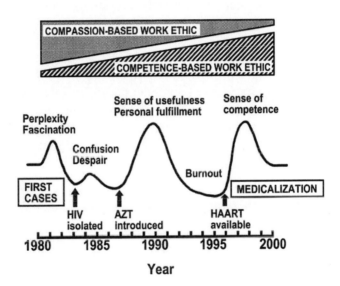

The wavy line indicates the emotional well-being of infectious diseases specialists during this period. In the beginning, the medical work ethic was primarily "compassion-based" because doctors lacked drugs and other technologies to do much for their patients. After HAART, the disease became "medicalized" and the work-ethic became primarily "competence-based." (See chapter COMPETENCE AND CARING.)

Beginning in 1981 the early cases left us fascinated but troubled and perplexed. What was it? What could we do for it? It was a grim novelty. We felt as though we'd been thrown back into medieval times—people were dying of a strange disease of which we knew little and for which we could do essentially nothing. As it became clear that we had on our hands a major epidemic, we became depressed. We became, perhaps for the first time, real *doctors* who made house calls, immersed ourselves in knotty social problems, and responded to the public demand for answers.

In 1983 isolation of the causative virus (now known as HIV) gave us the hope that help was on the way, but the patients kept coming and coming, dying and dying, and we became increasingly confused and despondent. The 1987 demonstration that the new drug AZT (now known as zidovudine) prolonged life excited us, like everyone else. But the epidemic still spread and its implications caused great public anxiety. Infectious diseases specialists were suddenly in great demand. Most of us became minor celebrities in our hometowns.

But the promise of AZT proved illusory—it bought patients about six months before the virus became resistant to it. More and more patients came and died. Many and perhaps most of us suffered from burnout. The intense research work—the utility— began to bear fruit. In late 1995 HAART became available. Suddenly the disease was eminently treatable. Provided they understood the disease and took their drugs faithfully, most people infected with HIV could lead near-normal lives. The disease had become "medicalized." Within the span of just 15 years, we'd gone from practicing "medieval medicine" to diagnosing and successfully managing the disease by using the most powerful tools of molecular biology!

In the beginning, we (that is, infectious diseases specialists) had little or no "competence" to offer, so we focused on caring at its highest levels including "compassion" in the sense of becoming fellow sufferers. We gave freely of our time. To various degrees we made significant sacrifices, and sometimes took personal risks, to care for sufferers from this devastating disease. The care ethic was primarily "compassion-based."

Later, the availability of HAART along with molecular tools for diagnosing and staging the disease made the care ethic primarily "competence-based." Patients no longer needed house calls. They no longer needed long emotional-support sessions, at least not from doctors. The focus of our anxieties began to shift. At first, we worried whether we were giving our patients enough emotional support. On a Sunday afternoon, for example, should we indulge in watching the second half of a pro football game or go out for nine holes of golf—or should we drive 30 miles into the country to see one of our dying patients whom we'd probably never see again? But later, and continuing into the present, our main concern centered on doing the best possible job at managing the various drugs and keeping watch for potential toxicities.

We do not wish on any of the readers of this *vade mecum* something as terrible as the HIV/AIDS epidemic. It's far better to absorb these take-home points just by reading about them. Still, we predict for all of you a life of "**novelty**, **utility**, and **charity**" beyond your wildest expectations, for they apply to most fields of medicine. We suspect that both individually and collectively you'll be up to the challenge of the Quest as you continue to absorb skills and knowledge and learn to apply them with wisdom and compassion.

COMPETENCE AND CARING:
THE TWIN PILLARS OF MEDICINE

Competence and caring are the pillars of medicine on which all else rests. William Osler sometimes dubbed these the "head and heart": **"As the practice of medicine is not a business and can never be one, the education of the heart—the moral side of the man—must keep pace with the education of the head. Our fellow creatures cannot be dealt with as [a] man deals in corn and coal; 'the human heart by which we live' must control our professional relationships."**[1] Medical educators and the general public have expressed concern that the U.S. healthcare system seemingly undermines in physicians qualities like empathy and altruism. We believe the rising importance of shared decision making will revive enthusiasm for knowing patients "through and through."

When anthropologist Margaret Mead was asked to name the first sign of civilization, she reportedly replied "a healed femur bone of a human being." Someone cared enough to stay with the wounded person and perhaps splint the limb, even though such attention went against the survival-of-the-fittest mentality of prehistoric peoples. Osler expressed a similar

---

[1] On the educational value of the medical society.

opinion: **"Medicine arose out of the primal sympathy of man with man; out of the desire to help those in sorrow, need and sickness . . . the instinct of self-preservation, the longing to relieve a loved one, and above all, the maternal passion . . . gradually softened the hard race of man."**[2]

But which matters more: competence or caring? Both are necessary, but our short answer is: Beneficent competence **is** caring, but "caring" without competence is fraud. A sick person can get caring from family, friends or even strangers, but a sick person engages a doctor who has special competence and training. As bioethicists Edmund Pellegrino and David Thomasma put it, "Nothing is more inconsistent with compassion than the well-meaning, empathetic but incompetent clinician."[3] Osler said similarly, **"In a well-arranged community a citizen should feel that he can at any time command the services of [a person] who has received a fair training in the science and art of medicine, into whose hands he may commit with safety the lives of those near and dear to him."**[4]

The definition of "competence" is straightforward: the power, ability, or capacity to perform a task or function. The definition of "caring" can be surprisingly problematic. "Caring" is often used as a general term, as in the familiar statement[5] by Harvard physician-educator Francis Weld Peabody: "One of the essential qualities of the clinician is interest in humanity, for the secret of the care of the patient is in caring for the patient." But at what level should caring take place?

It is possible to parse "caring" into several terms, based on their Greek or Latin roots, which in ascending order of difficulty are: beneficence, empathy, sympathy, and compassion (Table 1).

---

[2] *The Evolution of Modern Medicine*, 6-7.

[3] Pellegrino and Thomasma (1993), 83.

[4] The growth of a profession.

[5] Peabody (1927).

Table 1. CARING: A HIERARCHY OF TERMS		
TERM	**ROOT**	**ESSENCE**
Beneficence	Latin, *beneficentia*, "active kindness"	Doing good for someone else
Empathy	Greek, *en* ("in") plus *pathos* ("feeling")	Understanding (intellectually) how someone else feels
Sympathy	Greek, *sympatheia*, "like-feeling"	Experiencing feelings similar to someone else's
Compassion	Latin, *com* ("with") plus *pati* ("to suffer")	Becoming a fellow sufferer with someone else

Beneficence ("doing good") is caring at its most basic level. As such, it is now recognized as one of the four cornerstones of medical ethics (along with nonmaleficence [do not harm], justice, and autonomy) put forth by Beauchamp and Childress.[6] In 1902, Osler reminded members of the Canadian Medical Association that **"the profession of medicine is distinguished from all others by its *singular beneficence*. It alone does the work of charity in a Jovian and God-like way."**[7] Osler also stressed that physicians must have a high positive regard for humankind in general: **"To serve the art of medicine as it should be served, one must love his fellow man."**[8] Empathy now receives enormous attention in the

---

[6] Beauchamp and Childress (2012).

[7] Chauvinism in medicine.

[8] Address to the students of the Albany Medical College.

literature on medical education, and is considered a core competency, but what exactly is it?

It was not until 1958 that "empathy" (understanding and sharing how another person feels, while maintaining one's objectivity) and "sympathy" (affective response to another person, e.g., shedding tears) were clearly differentiated in the medical literature in a way that seems appropriate based on their Greek roots (Table 1). The Canadian neurosurgeon Wilder Penfield, who studied under Osler at Oxford recalled that Osler gave this clear message to medical students: "The motto of each of you as you undertake the examination and treatment of a case should be 'put yourself in his place.' Realize, so far as you can, the mental state of the patient, enter into his feelings, . . . scan gently his faults. The kindly word, the cheerful greeting, the sympathetic look all were part of Osler's bedside manner."[9]

"The physician," [runs the first aphorism of Hippocrates] "must not only be prepared to do what is right himself, but also to make the patient, the attendants, and externals cooperate." We see this principle today in the need for teamwork, and numerous studies correlate empathy with improved clinical outcomes. The patient and the other people with whom the physician must work are more likely to follow the directions of a doctor who seems to understand them.

The ascendancy of *shared decision making* will probably make empathy more important than ever in clinical medicine. However, it is possible that loss of empathy in medicine (as in other occupations that entail frequent emotionally-charged experiences, such as soldiers, firefighters, and policemen) may have a physiological basis. Neuroimaging studies indicate that

---

[9] Penfield (1949). Penfield was en route to England as a Rhodes Scholar in 1918 when his ship was torpedoed. He spent weeks recovering in Osler's home and got to know Osler better than most students.

gaining medical expertise causes a down-regulation in the sensory processing elicited by the perception of pain in others (the so-called "pain-empathy response").[10]

Being mindful of such influences is important during our training years.

Empathy and *concern* overlap, but they are not the same thing. On occasion we have opened a lecture to medical students on caring by asking for a show of hands to the question, "How many of you have ever been hospitalized for a major illness or operation?"

Usually only a few hands go up. When you are the patient, you quickly appreciate the kind of caring you get, and learn from it. You can also have the experience vicariously, as in the 1991 movie *The Doctor,* in which a hugely-successful, egotistical surgeon (played by William Hurt) discovers empathy only after a bout with throat cancer. It showed well how serious illness can affect a doctor's values and approach to patients. Many similar narratives by physicians[11] relate how serious illness made them appreciate the dehumanizing forces embedded in our health care systems and thereby enhanced their ability to empathize with patients.

Not wishing life-threatening illness on anyone, we suggest that the best approach continues to be to listen attentively to the patient's narrative. This takes time, which most of us find to be in short supply, but it pays rich dividends.

The term "compassion" is, in our opinion, used all too casually. As the writer Flannery O'Connor put it: "Compassion is a word that sounds good in anybody's mouth ... It's a quality which no one can put his finger on in any exact critical sense, so it is always

---

[10] Decety et al (2010).

[11] Kempainen et al (2007).

safe for anybody to use." Our objection to such common use is that "compassion" from its Latin roots literally means *to be a fellow sufferer,* to bear another's burdens to one's own disadvantage. Such responses are beyond the usual call of duty.

An example happened to JBV. I was a surgeon, married to a nurse, at a time when my four-year-old son Joey was seriously injured in an auto crash, suffering a brain stem injury and requiring a laparotomy, a cystostomy and a tracheostomy. When he was recovered enough for discharge we brought him home, but he still required a lot of care, suctioning every two hours at night, for example, that continued for several weeks. It was stressful for us, despite our medical background, and we were getting burned out.

One afternoon the doorbell rang. At the door was a couple who had cared for Joey—she was head nurse in the pediatric ICU and he was an anesthesiologist—and they handed over two tickets to the theater, saying, "We can take care of Joey just as well as you—and you need a break! Go out to dinner and see this show." It was a memorable and welcome example of *compassion*.

Summing up, here are some suggestions for medical students and young physicians:

- Understand the various levels of caring.
- Make the acquisition of competence your first priority, but pay close attention to how you care for patients, and how they respond to you.
- Develop your own style of caring, which, in turn, will be based on your own personality makeup, and let it enhance, not diminish, your relations to your patients.
- Make empathy a habit. In non-emergency situations, seek to establish rapport with your patients. Try to understand

what illness and suffering mean to each one as you care for them.

"Do the kind thing and do it first"—that, it was said,[12] seemed to be Osler's unwritten model.

---

[12] MKR (2016).

MEDICAL PROFESSIONALISM

In Osler's day—the end of the 19th century and into the early 20th century—little was written about medical professionalism, perhaps because the three "learned professions"—the Law, the Clergy, and Medicine—were well respected. These were characterized by their special academic preparation and by their *fiduciary* obligations, namely a bond of trust, which meant that the attorney, the pastor, and the physician put the interest of their client, their parishioner, or their patient *ahead* of their own interests.

Since Osler's time, vast changes in society, government, business and advertising have occurred. The profession of medicine has not been unaffected. In the field of academic medicine over the past three decades, many articles, books and conferences have dealt with "Medical Professionalism," and the concept has slowly evolved. The thrust of many of the earlier efforts was to re-emphasize that *putting the patient's interests ahead of one's own is the core of professionalism.* The American Board of Internal Medicine (ABIM) defined six elements of professionalism (**altruism, accountability, excellence, duty, honor, and integrity**) and seven signs and symptoms of betrayal of professionalism (**abuse of power, arrogance, greed,**

misrepresentation, impairment, lack of conscientiousness, and conflict of interest).[1]

Consider this thought experiment: What do you see happening in society—and in medicine, too—as you ponder the six elements listed above and reflect on our leaders? Do likewise for the seven symptoms of betrayal as we witness them through the media. Do you find it humbling how far we have strayed from these ideals? As students and physicians, we want to promote the "good six" and avoid and resist the "bad seven." It is not easy.

At least three societal trends complicate these and other serious efforts to define, foster, and measure medical professionalism. First, there is a perceived clash of cultures between traditional professional values and the values of government and business. Professionalism is diminished when employment conditions and regulations diminish doctors' autonomy and create a complex web of conflicting obligations and interests. (Most of the recent literature on medical professionalism underscores what *physicians* should do, while ignoring what *society* must do to allow to the fullest flowering of medical professionalism. Marketplace values—for example, profit, competition, consumerism, short-term goals, creating demand through advertising, and seeking power through monopoly—diametrically oppose professionalism in the traditional sense.)

The second trend (a corollary to the first) is the expectation of many and perhaps most of today's medical students and residents that they will be *employees* in a health care system. Two physicians[2] recently reviewed the potential impact of various clauses in contracts on medical professionalism as summarized in Table 1.

---

[1] www.ncbi.nlm.nih.gov/pubmed/1206
[2] Poses and Smith (2016).

Table 1. SOME CHALLENGES TO PROFESSIONALISM POSED BY CLAUSES IN PHYSICIANS' CONTRACTS*

TYPE OF CLAUSE	POTENTIAL IMPACT ON PROFESSIONALISM
Termination without cause clauses; and confidentiality clauses	Such clauses might dissuade physicians from complaining about unethical behavior, malfeasance (deviations from the usual and customary standard of care), quality, and safety.
Productivity-incentive clauses	Such clauses might encourage physicians to over utilize or underutilize (depending on employers' financial interests) diagnostic procedures or treatments. Also, clauses such as reimbursement by relative-value units (RVUs) may pressure physicians to "do more in less time," cutting corners.
Clauses restricting outside activities	Such clauses might restrict freedom of speech, academic freedom, and teaching and research opportunities.
Non-compete clauses	Such clauses might hinder physician's ability to leave positions they find unsatisfactory and to practice elsewhere in the vicinity, which may deprive patients of local expertise.
"Leakage-control" clauses	Such clauses, by discouraging referrals outside the employer's system, may reduce quality of care for individual patients.

*Modified after Poses and Smith (2016).

Perhaps the most pernicious are "blanket confidentiality clauses" that may "bury evidence of poor quality or safety problems, choke whistleblowers, or conceal mismanagement and malfeasance." Also, "termination without cause" may include termination for "disruptive behavior" that could be broadly defined to include dissenting with management, or whistle blowing about ethical or quality issues. These authors grimly conclude: "Ascendant market fundamentalism (also called *neoliberalism*) has pressured physicians to become <u>*business persons*</u> rather than professionals." [Emphasis added] In fairness we should add that many health system employers including large networks strive to safeguard medical professionalism by collaborating openly and transparently with physicians and other employees.

New York Times columnist David Brooks observed[3] that in essence there are two lenses—the economic lens or the moral lens—that people can use to view any situation. The economic lens says people are motivated by self-interest, seeking "What's in it for me?" The moral lens considers the greater good, looking beyond self to the good of society. We believe that as medical professionals (called **"Pros"** in the paragraphs below) we should be altruistic, viewing through the moral lens.

Here are some practical aspects of being a **Pro** from experiences that we have found worth imparting to students and residents:

- **Pros** are readily available when on call. (I recall one time when on the firing line in the ED I tried to get hold of the internist on backup call for us, to admit an unassigned patient, only to be told by the doctors' exchange that he was signed out to the ED!)

---

[3] Brooks (2016).

- **Pros** give patients their undivided attention. (On occasion I have accompanied friends or relatives to their doctor appointments and have been discouraged to see a doctor thumbing through the chart or facing away typing, not listening closely to the patient.) Try to minimize interruptions. Don't multitask!

- **Pros** add "hooks" to the chart to aid memory for follow-up visits and to personalize their care. (Once when I returned to my surgeon after an operation, his opening question was "How's that son of yours doing?" I was surprised and pleased that he remembered my son had been injured in an auto accident, so I asked him how he remembered that minor fact. He shared that he jotted down such little items of interest on the chart to prompt his memory and personalize his practice. I began to do that, too.)

- **Pros** run on time! If you are delayed or late, let your office know so patients can choose to re-schedule. Their time is as valuable as yours. To think otherwise is arrogance. Osler asserted that punctuality was the prime essential of a physician.[4]

- **Pros** don't do drugs. **Pros** are not compromised or controlled by drugs or alcohol. Shun alcohol when on call. Our patients need our best and clearest attention.

- Finally, and critically, a **Pro** always does his or her best job even when he or she doesn't *feel* like it! (CSB)

---

[4] Holman (1969).

Much of Osler's counsel to students related to issues of professionalism. He memorably said, **"The practice of medicine is an art, not a trade; a calling, not a business; a calling in which your heart will be exercised equally with your head."**[5] He saw spending the last few minutes of the day reading in a bedside library as a way to exercise the heart.

(See also Appendix C: A Bedside Library.)

---

[5] The master-word in medicine.

ETIQUETTE

In the hustle-bustle and hurry-scurry of modern life, it is easy to overlook the small things that make life a bit easier and more pleasant for those with whom we dwell. Dealing with sick people who are not often their best selves, with administrators, fellow health care workers, and families who make just claims on our time can be taxing; we may find it hard to behave as we might in a relaxed social situation. Osler commented, **"It must be confessed that the practice of medicine among our fellow creatures is often a testy and choleric business."**[1] Yet he was known for his evenness of temper (his equanimity, which he wrote about in his essay titled "Aequanimitas"), and for his cheery disposition. He had a broad view of human nature and was tolerant of others: **"One of the first essentials in securing good-natured equanimity is not to expect too much of the people amongst whom you dwell . . . Deal gently then with this deliciously credulous old human nature in which we work, and restrain your indignation."**[2]

Osler believed in living the Golden Rule—treating others as you'd wish to be treated. More recently it's

---

[1] Chauvinism in medicine.

[2] Aequanimitas.

been expanded to the Platinum Rule: *Treat others as they themselves would like to be treated*,[3] which is good advice as we care for sick and suffering patients. Osler believed and exemplified this when he asserted **"the physician needs a clear head and a kind heart; his work is arduous and complex, requiring the exercise of the very highest faculties of the mind, while constantly appealing to the emotions and finer feelings."**[4]

When the present authors were medical students there was a popular song entitled "Little Things Mean a Lot." They do, indeed, and they can be an important factor in our relations with our patients and families. This was brought out in a recent book authored by AOS member Barry Silverman, *Your Doctor's Manners Matter: Better Health through Civility in the Doctor's Office and in the Hospital*.[5] Here are some suggestions for common courtesy when making rounds:

- Ask the patient's permission to enter the room. Knock on the door and wait for an answer. Make sure your ID badge is turned so that your name and position are clearly visible. Enter and introduce yourself.
- Proceed to the hand-hygiene-agent dispenser or to the sink, and lather up. Then, turn to the patient and others in the room as you dry your hands.
- Explain your role in the patient's care. Make eye contact with the patient and with others in the room. If family, relatives, and/or friends are present, ascertain their relationships to the patient. Touch the patient, using either a handshake or "fist bump," wearing gloves if

---

[3] Alessandra and O'Connor (1996).

[4] Teaching and thinking.

[5] Silverman and Adler (2014).

necessary. (You can learn a lot as you take the pulse and feel the temperature of a patient's hand.)

- *Sit down. This puts you at eye level with your patient.* This is extremely important. It is a common courtesy but too often neglected by doctors. Sitting down need not prolong the visit, but abundant anecdotal experience suggests that patients believe that you've spent more time with them if you sit, rather than stand. (Besides, standing conveys the impression that you're planning your exit even as you talk to them!)
- As you prepare to leave the room, lather up again and share your plans and offer words of encouragement.

Osler was known for his bedside teaching and his bedside manner. He asserted its importance in two addresses:[6]

> **Kindliness of disposition and gentleness of manners are qualities essential in a practitioner. If they do not exist naturally, they are virtues which must be cultivated if not assumed. The rough voice, the hard sharp answer, and the blunt matter are as much out of place in the hospital ward as in 'any lady's boudoir.' . . . The kindly word, the cheerful greeting, the sympathetic look, trivial [though] they may seem, help to brighten the paths of the poor sufferers and are often as "oil and wine" to the bruised spirits entrusted to our care[7] . . . Remember that every patient upon whom you wait will examine you critically and form an estimate of you by the way**

---

[6] Unpublished draft of an 1885 address to medical students at the Penn; and a Valedictory Address to the graduates in medicine and surgery at McGill.

[7] A reference to the Good Samaritan's roadside care in Luke 10:34.

in which you conduct yourself at the bedside. Skill and nicety in manipulation, whether in the simple act of feeling the pulse or in the performance of any minor operation will do more towards establishing confidence in you, than a string of Diplomas, or the reputation of extensive Hospital experience.

Osler's point is sometimes paraphrased: "They don't care how much you know until they know how much you care."[8]

It is worth mentioning here the ***impact that our words*** can have at the bedside. Dr. Bernard Lown, (who, besides being an outstanding cardiologist who invented the cardioverter, also was recipient of the Nobel Peace Prize[9] for his efforts toward world peace) tells an interesting story:[10]

At one morning rounds I commented to the attending staff that Mr. B. had a wholesome, very loud third-sound gallop. Everyone dutifully auscultated the heart and nodded ascent. (Actually, a third-sound gallop is a poor sign and denotes that the heart muscle is straining and usually failing.) The patient had an oxygen mask and seemingly was unmindful of the dialogue across the bed, peppered as it was with medical jargon. [But] slowly and quite unexpectedly he improved and eventually was discharged from the hospital.

Some months later, when I saw him for an office checkup, I marveled at his recovery and asked about the basis for the miraculous improvement. "Doctor, I

---

[8] Kahn (2008).

[9] Lown accepted the Nobel Prize on behalf of the group he co-founded, the International Physicians for the Prevention of Nuclear War.

[10] Lown (1983).

not only know what got me better," he said, "but even the exact moment when it happened. I was sure the end was near and that you and your staff had given up hope. However, Thursday morning when you entered with your troops, something happened that changed everything. You listened to my heart; you seemed pleased with the findings and announced to all those standing about my bed that I had a 'wholesome gallop.' I knew that the doctors, in talking to me, might try to soften things, but I knew they wouldn't kid each other. So when I overheard you tell your colleagues that I had a wholesome gallop, I figured I still had a lot of kick to my heart and could not be dying. My spirits were for the first time lifted and I knew I would live and recover."

In this same introduction to this book, Lown shares another story about the power of words at the bedside, this time the casual comment on rounds by the famous Harvard clinician, Samuel Levine, that "This woman has TS" as he left the room. He meant she had tricuspid stenosis. But the patient thought it meant *Terminal Situation*, and from that very moment her condition deteriorated and she went rapidly downhill and died with massive pulmonary edema. "To this day," Lown wrote (he was the resident on the case) "the recollection of this tragic happening causes me to tremble at the awesome power of the physician's word." Lown—age ninety-six in 2016—has written a book about medical practice worth reading by every student.[11]

How you behave with your patients will impact your practice and your reputation. Norman Cousins,[12] while on the faculty of

---

[11] Lown (1996).

[12] Cousins was for over thirty years the Editor of the *Saturday Review of Literature* and thereafter was an adjunct professor in the medical school at UCLA. His several books that

UCLA conducted and published a survey of 1500 patients about whether they had changed physicians or had contemplated doing so, and published the results in the *New England Journal of Medicine*. The results were instructive. Here is what he wrote in his book *Head First: The Biology of Hope*:[13]

> The most startling figure that turned up was that 85% of the respondents reported that they had either changed physicians in the past five years or were thinking of changing now. Equally startling were the reasons behind the change. When these reasons were tabulated, we discovered that people took knowledge for granted, that was what a medical diploma signified. Beyond that diploma, however, were other factors that counted heavily with patients. The questionnaire revealed that most people changed physicians not for reasons of competence but because of the doctor's style or office manner. They were troubled by insensitivity to their needs, or poor communication techniques, or by lack of respect for the patient's views, or by overemphasis on technology.

The importance of etiquette also extends to how physicians should deal with each other; it has been of concern to the profession for generations. The original code of ethics by the American Medical Association in 1847 dealt more with etiquette than with ethics because strife between doctors was not uncommon (See Appendix D for the Modernized AMA Code of Ethics). Osler, however, was known as a peacemaker. He promoted local,

---

relate his bouts with illness in his life are instructive for students and residents.
[13] Cousins (1989).

regional, and national medical societies where physicians could enjoy camaraderie and learn others' perspectives. He had two hard and fast rules, as valid today as when he asserted them: Never criticize a colleague openly and never believe a patient's criticism of a colleague.[14]

---

[14] Unity, peace and concord.

GENDER EQUALITY AND DIVERSITY

When the authors of this *vade mecum* were medical students, women were a distinct minority. For example, of the six women in JBV's class of 72 students at the University of Rochester, three dropped out and three married classmates. Contrast that with 30 years later when women comprised half of his daughter's class at Oregon. But although today women comprise half of U.S. medical school graduates, gender inequality persists in the medicine, particularly in academia: Although men and women enter the career pipeline at similar rates, academic medicine does not equivalently advance them. Currently, women account for 32% of associate professors, 20% of full professors, 14% of department chairs and 11% of deans at U.S medical schools—far from the gender parity seen in the number of medical students at most schools since the 1990s.[1] The authors of another study concluded, "Faculty men and women are equally engaged in their work and share similar leadership aspirations. However, medical schools have failed to create and sustain an environment where women feel fully accepted and supported to succeed."[2]

---

[1] Kaatz and Carnes (2014).

[2] Pololi (2013).

What was Osler's take on women in medicine? There were no women in his medical school class at McGill. It was thought by many medical educators at the time that pursuing medicine was an arduous course for women. Osler was an early champion of women. When he addressed the Canadian Medical Association in 1885, he said, **"My sympathies are entirely with them in the attempt to work out the problem as to how far they can succeed in such an arduous profession as that of medicine."**[3]

Six years later Osler was chief of medicine at the new Johns Hopkins University School of Medicine, which had pledged to admit women on the same basis as men. (That stipulation came at the insistence of a group of determined Baltimore women led by Mary Elizabeth Garrett, who raised the additional $100,000 that was essential to the school's opening.) At that outset, Osler attested to the favorable performance of women medical students in Switzerland and Paris, and elaborated:

> **How far it may be expedient to encourage women to enter the medical profession, the work of which is often disagreeable and always laborious, is a question which receives very diverse answers; but the right of women to study medicine is now granted on all sides. . . . If any woman feels that the medical profession is her vocation, no obstacle should be placed in the way of her obtaining the best possible education, and every facility should be offered, so that, as a practitioner, she should have a fair start in the race.**[4]

---

[3] The growth of a profession.

[4] On the opening of the Johns Hopkins Medical School to women. The first class at the Johns Hopkins University School of Medicine contained three women, about whom Osler allegedly quipped after the first year that "one-third dropped out and one-third married their professors." There are stories, perhaps apocryphal, that Osler told Dorothy Reed (a future scientist known eponymously for the Reed-Sternberg cell of Hodgkin's

Osler's most ardent admirers included prominent women physicians. Dr. Maude Abbott, a Canadian physician who became a leading expert on congenital heart disease and who with Osler co-founded the International Association of Medical Museums in 1906, edited a large volume of reminiscences[5] about Osler that provides much of what we know about Osler's personal characteristics. Dr. Claribel Cone of Baltimore described Osler's "rare personality and all those high qualities of mind and heart that go to make the ideal physician and teacher," and, in words that hint of her identity as one of the nation's earliest collectors of the French Impressionists, described making ward rounds with "the Chief": "He was the artist, and with master-strokes he would limn for us case after case. In words rare as they were beautiful; in phrases pregnant with meaning, in manner—at times droll, again almost divine in its subtle suggestion of sympathy—he would assemble the essential facts of each case and create a masterpiece as rich in suggestion, as universal in appeal as a Giotto, a Rembrandt, or a Giorgione."[6] Who would not wish to have made ward rounds with William Osler?

Osler's biographer Michael Bliss summarizes: "Compared with most of his colleagues, Osler was fairly progressive on the medical women question."[7] Osler's crowning remark on the potential of women in medicine came in 1907 during a eulogy to the memory of Dr. Mary Putnam Jacobi, a physician, a suffragist, and advocate for women's health:

---

disease) to "turn back" on her first day of medical school, and that it was he who made the motion that denied graduation to the subsequently-famous literary and cultural icon Gertrude Stein.

[5] Abbott (1926).

[6] Cone (1926).

[7] Bliss (1999), 148.

For years I have been waiting the advent of the modern Trotula,[8] a woman in the profession with an intellect so commanding that she will rank with the Harveys, the Hunters, and Pasteurs; the Virchows, and the Listers. That she has not yet arisen is no

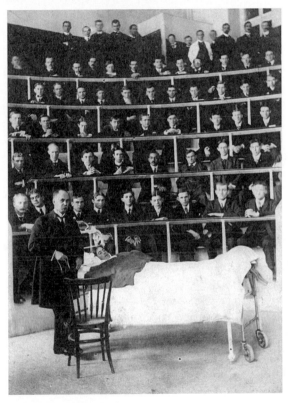

Osler conducting a clinic at McGill University in 1906. Note that there are no women in the class.

---

[8] Trotula was a 12th century woman physician of Salerno, Italy.

reflection on the small band of women physicians who have joined our ranks in the last fifty years. Stars of the first magnitude are rare, but that such a one will arise among women physicians I have not the slightest doubt. And let us be thankful that when she comes she will not have to waste her precious energies in the worry of a struggle for recognition.

Osler's vision of a modern Trotula was fulfilled at Johns Hopkins some thirty years after his death in the person of pediatric cardiologist Dr. Helen Taussig, who with surgeon Alfred Blalock, designed the "blue baby" operation to treat Tetralogy of Fallot. Taussig also recognized the birth defect damage (phocomelia) caused in Europe by the sedative drug thalidomide. Her testimony before the FDA succeeded in having it banned from the American market. She received the Lasker Award in 1954 and ten years later from President Lyndon Johnson received the Medal of Freedom.

A recent article[9] in the *ACS Bulletin* addressed ongoing challenges for women in surgery and emphasized the valuable role of senior surgical women mentors. One student commented that one of her mentors led by example in the caring way she interacted with her patients and with her expertise in the operating room. "She spent time teaching me to tie knots late on a Friday night, while inviting discussion about the pros and cons of a career in surgery . . . One of my chief residents was a wife, mother of two daughters and future transplant surgeon. She pushed me to make my presentations more concise, precise, and accurate. She taught me to suture, [and] I hope one day to emulate her as both a surgeon and a teacher." Mentoring in medicine and surgery is an

---

9   Grassi C et al (2016).

important factor in education and in making a choice of further training. (See also the chapter on Mentors and Mentoring.) Racial equality and LGBT equality are as important as gender issues to medical students and medical professionals nowadays.[10]

As regards our sister profession, the Law, we were struck by the relevance of what Supreme Court Justice Ruth Bader Ginsburg said in the preface to her book *My Own Words*:[11]

> Earlier, I spoke of great changes I have seen in women's occupations. Yet one must acknowledge the still bleak part of the picture. Most people in poverty in the United States and the world over are women and children, women's earnings here and abroad trail the earnings of men with comparable educations and experience, our workplaces do not adequately accommodate the demands of child bearing and childrearing, and we have yet to devise effective ways to ward off sexual harassment at work and domestic violence in our homes. I am optimistic, however, that movement toward enlistment of the talent of all who compose "We the People," will continue.

DIVERSITY among students and practitioners is an issue that is increasingly gaining prominence, one that was not addressed at all in Osler's day. As one observer put it, "the discrepancy between the demographics of doctors and the people in the communities we serve" needs attention by society and the medical community. There is a paucity of underrepresented minority groups within medicine and surgery, and our civic population will best be

---

[10] Personal communication from Rutgers student Michael John Sylvester, 14 November 2016.

[11] Ginsburg RB (2016), xviii.

served if we can achieve a more equitable balance.[12] The medical schools of this nation continue to build diverse classes across a number of racial and ethnic backgrounds. More than 2,000 Hispanic, Latino, or people of Spanish origin enrolled in medical school in 2016, and the number of black and African Americans enrollees surpassed 1,700. In addition, more than 5,400 Hispanic, Latino, or individuals of Spanish origin, and nearly 5,000 black or African-American students applied to medical school this year.[13] With proper mindfulness and funding, this issue—across all levels of education—will follow the lead taken in addressing gender issues in the profession.

---

[12] Personal communication in November, 2016, from Mary McGrath, president-elect of the American College of Surgeons.

[13] AAMC Video on diversity released 1 November 2016. See Internet Sources.

MEDICINE AND THE NEW MILLENNIUM

I n 1999 the editors of *The Lancet* in planning a supplement issue to greet the new millennium invited the French medical historian Danielle Gourevitch to write on "The history of medical teaching."[1] Gourevitch called Osler "the last *maître à penser* for a noble-minded general medicine." (The French term *maître à penser*, translated literally as "master of thinking," denotes a teacher who, beyond imparting facts and points of view, shows us how to think for ourselves or, more broadly, to manage the complexities and ambiguities of the human condition.) She saw no point in teaching the humanities to medical students. She saw a bright future for medicine (that is, for health care) but a bleak future for the medical profession. She wrote:

> Today's technical and dehumanized medicine has no past, has no cultural language, has no philosophy . . . . The year 2000 will witness the triumph of medicine, but also the substitution of doctors by health technicians. I do not believe in the pretense of teaching literature to first-year medical students. . . . Doctors should intellectually chase nascent science; alas, the messages of seminars generally have no other aim than cost containment in health care.

---

[1] Gourevitch (1999).

Under these circumstances, one wonders whether doctors really need an academic training.

Gourevitch implied that the broadly-educated physician who brings to the clinic or bedside wisdom gleaned from the humanities has little or no place in today's technology-heavy health care system. The future belongs to health care technicians, she asserted.

Gourevitch is not alone in her guarded prognosis for the medical profession. Sociologists such as Paul Starr in *The Social Transformation of American Medicine*[2] and Alan Krause in *Death of the Guilds*[3] have been making similar predictions for years. Starr foresaw "the coming of the MBAs" (masters of business administration) as a threat to physicians' autonomy. Krause concluded that the twin forces of government and capitalism have undermined the professions throughout the Western democracies during the twentieth century, with the medical profession in the U.S. being the most extreme case of rise and fall. Nor do such prognoses emanate entirely from critics outside of medicine. Consider, for example, books by pediatrician John Lantos (*Do We Still Need Doctors?*) and cardiologist Eric Topol (*The Creative Destruction of Medicine*; *The Patient Will See You Now*). More broadly, sociologists point out that *all* professionals—not just physicians—are at risk of being "slowly transformed into especially privileged technical workers."[4] Let's try to fit today's challenges into historical context.

In 2010 the ethicist Nuala Kenny, addressing the AOS, identified four pivotal events in the evolution of today's medical profession (Table 1).

---

[2] Starr (1982).

[3] Krause (1996).

[4] Friedson E (2001), 209-10.

Table 1. FOUR PIVOTAL EVENTS IN THE EVOLUTION OF THE MEDICAL PROFESSION*			
EVENT	**DATES**	**SIGNIFICANCE**	
The Hippocratic tradition	5th-Century B.C. Greece and 2nd-Century A.D. Rome	Insistence on medicine based on objective evidence as opposed to superstition, religion, and magic; adoption and promotion of Hippocratic medicine by early Christians who welcomed a system of medicine that did not have a competing belief system to theirs.	
The invention and adoption of medical ethics	18th-Century Great Britain and 19th-Century United States	Insistence on a system of ethics in which the patient's interests transcend the provider's, notably by John Gregory (who was influenced by David Hume's concept of sympathy) and Thomas Percival; adoption of a formal code of ethics by the American Medical Association in 1947 (the world's first).	
The Flexner Report	1910 (United States)	Insistence on "a more uniformly arduous and expensive medical education" with rigorous requirements for admission to medical school and rigorous training in the basic sciences; stimulation of the growth of large full-time faculties. Less-rigorous, "proprietary" schools closed throughout the U.S.	
Commercialization and commoditization of medicine	Late-20th-Century Western societies, continuing to the present day	Will this eliminate professionalism as previously developed, taught, and practiced? Will physicians become increasingly subservient to a consumer-driven business model of health-care delivery? Medicine is increasingly seen as a commodity to be bought and sold like any other.	

*Modified after Kenny (2010).

Each of the first three of these events elevated the status of physicians, but the fourth—the commercialization and commoditization of medicine that is taking place right now—represents a clash of cultures with the following consequences:

- Confusion regarding the relative roles of physicians and patients.
- A complex web of conflicts of interests and obligations.
- Reduced trust in the physician's judgment.
- Decreased moral responsibility and accountability of the physician.
- Loss of the physician's ability to make recommendations on the basis of potential benefit versus potential harm.
- Devaluation of whatever cannot be objectively measured.
- More reliance on technology and less reliance on thoughtful judgment.

She concluded that today's commercialization and commoditization of medicine might even eliminate the possibility of professionalism.[5]

How would Osler respond? He would probably respond with his characteristic optimism, reminding us that change brings opportunities. He would probably tell us that our best security rests in adherence to principles and ideals traceable to the Hippocratic ideal of love of both science and humanity (*philotechnia* and *philanthropia*). Osler, we believe, would encourage us to adjust to new conditions of practice without compromising ideals, values, and principles. He would acknowledge that young people of the early twenty-first century are entitled to manage their

---

[5] Kenny (2010).

lives differently than did prior generations, according to their preferences and lifestyles.

Generalizing about generations is, of course, simplistic. Recorded history documents little if any change in human nature. Study, for example, the Hebrew Bible (Old Testament) or Plutarch's *Lives*—you'll find characters not unlike those all around you!

Sociologists agree that successive generations develop distinctive characteristics and values as adaptations to the prevailing social environments of their formative years. On that basis, physicians born after 1965, for example, tend to see things differently than their predecessors. (Table 2 details some values and characteristics of recent generations, allowing comparisons between them and showing some of the implications for medicine.)

Finally, Osler would tell us that the phrase "I entered a profession and left a business" is not new; rather, it is the traditional jeremiad of the newly-retired. He might encourage younger physicians to use today's social media to assume (as historian Rosemary Stevens puts it[6]) "a new position of moral leadership in American health care." Ever the optimist, Osler would agree that while today's challenges are great, so are the opportunities.

Will the dire predictions about the commercialization of medical practice and the triumph of technology cited above come true? We certainly hope not! A lot will depend on the character of those who are teaching and learning medicine. In many respects, the future will be in your hands, students and residents!

---

[6]   Stevens R (2001).

Table 2. GENERALIZATIONS ABOUT THE VALUES AND CHARACTERISTICS OF LIVING GENERATIONS AND THEIR IMPLICATIONS FOR MEDICINE

GENERA-TION	BIRTH YEARS	CHARACTERISTICS & VALUES	IMPLICATIONS FOR MEDICINE
Veterans	Before 1946	They value discipline, law, order, & stability; they are trusting, respectful, hopeful, and loyal; Generally they are uncomfortable with change	These are traditionalist physicians who view their profession as a constant, uninterrupted calling; they focus on professionalism and duty
Baby Boomers	1946-1964	Value job status, job security, and social standing; are more critical, assertive, and demanding than Veterans	Although similar to traditionalist physicians on the surface, place more value on status and tangible rewards

Gen. X	1965-1979	Resourceful, individu-alistic, self-reliant, and skeptical of authority; place less value on corporate loyalty and status symbols	Value being a physician as only one part of their identity; seek a balanced life but also security; often change employers
Gen. Y	1980-1994	Technologically aware; comfortable with ethnic diversity; values similar to Veterans; strong sense of morality	Expect "employment model" with limited, self-defined hours and limited patient-care responsibilities
Gen. Z (Presently, or soon in medical school—will be our future leaders)	1995-	Internet-dependent, technology-savvy, valuing on-line resources and social media such as Google, Twitter, MySpace, Linked-in, and Facebook	To be determined, but have the potential for encouraging globalized value systems and fostering positive change through Internet-based collaborations

THE VIRTUES IN MEDICINE

THE INFLUENCE OF VIRTUOUS CHARACTER

The preface to the first edition (1950) of Harrison's *Principles of Internal Medicine* begins thus: "No greater opportunity, responsibility, or obligation can fall to the lot of a human being than to become a physician. In the care of the suffering, he[1] needs technical skill, scientific knowledge, and human understanding. He who uses these with courage, with humility, and with wisdom will provide a unique service for his fellow man and will build an enduring edifice of character within himself."

Osler spoke of "the silent influence of character on character" as gleaned from lifelong study of the humanities:

> **In the records of no other profession** [than medicine] **is there to be found so large a number** [of individuals] **who have combined intellectual pre-eminence with nobility of character. The higher education so much needed to-day is not given in the school, is not to be bought in the marketplace, but it**

---

[1] Harrison et al (1950), 1-5. Sixty-six years later, with women comprising half of medical school graduating classes, Dr. Tinsley Harrison would doubtless eschew the masculine pronoun!

**has to be wrought out in each one of us for himself;
it is the silent influence of character on character and
in no way more potent than in the contemplation of
the lives of the great and good of the past, in no way
more than that in 'the touch divine of noble natures
gone.'"[2]**

Toward the close of the twentieth century a group of
American psychologists initiated the "Values in Action
Classification Project"[3] with the aim of identifying identifiable
character strengths—a guide to identifying "what's right with
people"—as opposed to the *Diagnostic and Statistical Manual
of Mental Disorders* for identifying "what's wrong with people."
They concluded that throughout history cultures have endorsed
six clusters of character strengths that correspond precisely to
the seven classical virtues of antiquity. The authors of this *vade
mecum* believe that focusing on those seven virtues offers a
starting point for building character.

If we define character as *the propensity to do the right thing
amid difficult circumstances,* then building character becomes
one of the most important goals of medical education. Medicine
at its best is a moral enterprise, and will be influenced by persons
behaving virtuously.

We will discuss virtues as they relate to physicians and the
practice of medicine based on the four "cardinal virtues" (described
by Plato in *The Republic* [Wisdom, Justice, Temperance and
Courage] and the three "transcendent virtues" [Faith, Hope and
Love] (described by St. Paul in First Corinthians, Chapter 13).

---

[2] Books and men.

[3] Peterson and Seligman (2004).

Table 1. THE SEVEN CLASSICAL VIRTUES OF ANTIQUITY, AND SOME OF THEIR "SUB-VIRTUES"

Category	Virtue	Sub-Virtues*
The four Cardinal Virtues (after Plato, *The Republic*)	Wisdom	Caution, creativity, critical thinking, curiosity, foresight, ingenuity, interest, judgment, love of learning, open-mindedness, originality, perspective, practical intelligence, prudence, and self-transcendence
	Justice	Citizenship, conscience, duty, ethical sophistication, equity, fairness, honesty, leadership, loyalty, mercy, respect for others, social responsibility, teamwork
	Temperance	Caution, contentment, discretion, emotional control, forgiveness, humility, mercy, moderation, modesty, purity, prudence, self-control, self-regulation, simplicity
	Courage	Altruism, bravery, energy, enthusiasm, honesty, idealism, industriousness, perseverance, self-invention, valor, vitality, zest
The three Transcendent Virtues (after St. Paul, First Corinthians 13:13)	Faith	Awe, faith, gratitude, humor (philosophical), playfulness, purpose, religiousness, reverence, spirituality, trust, wonder
	Hope	Future-mindedness, goal setting, optimism, prayer, sense of meaning, and purpose
	Love	Beneficence, charity, compassion, empathy, friendship, generosity, kindness, nurturance, and politeness

*These sub-virtues, listed here alphabetically rather than in order of importance, are taken largely from the positive psychology movement, and especially from the work of Peterson and Seligman (2004).

Table 1 sets forth the seven virtues and lists some of the sub-virtues that spin off from them. In the following seven sections of this manual we discuss and explore each of the seven as they relate to the character of the physician and to the practice of medicine. As you peruse and ponder these last sections, we suggest:

Memorize the four cardinal virtues and three transcendent virtues[4] and consider the sub-virtues as they impact our lives in medicine.

Develop a habit of ethical reflection. After you have encountered a tough situation, review (1) the facts; (2) the virtues that might apply; and (3) the principles, values, and external considerations that might apply. Then, contemplate how you would handle a similar situation in the future.

Ask yourself: With today's emphasis on patient autonomy and clinical outcomes, does the "character" of the doctor still matter? (Most ethicists would say yes, at least to the extent that the balance of power between doctor and patient tilts toward the doctor.) We believe it does.

Read edifying literature, including the classics, with the aim of absorbing what William Osler called **"the silent influence of character on character."**[5] Seek also to find how virtuous behavior influences the encounter between you and your patients and your colleagues.

---

[4] Although the terminology for the transcendent virtues derives from Christianity, their content and value cut across all religions and the secular world as well.

[5] Bean (1950), 140.

COURAGE

A mong Plato's four cardinal virtues COURAGE is the most universally admired, and is the stuff of myth and legends, the inspiration for some of the world's best stories. Winston Churchill ranked courage first among the cardinal virtues because it makes the others possible. Courage requires temperance, for it is the mean between foolhardiness and cowardice.

Physicians often display courage in literature and history. An example of the former is Dr. Bernard Rieux in Albert Camus' novel *The Plague*, who remains at his post amid the epidemic in Oran, despite the risk of contracting the lethal disease. A fictional character, his example has been mirrored in reality by many physicians who continue to visit the sick despite the risk of exposure to infectious, contagious diseases. An example from history—in this case courage going beyond the call of duty—would be Major James Carroll, a U.S. army physicians who allowed himself to get bitten by an infected mosquito to prove it carried and transmitted yellow fever in Cuba in 1900.

The HIV/AIDS epidemic stirred much debate in the medical community over the question whether physicians and other health care workers were ethically required to risk blood exposure. Most accepted the risk, and a few contracted the disease. The arrival of effective drugs, enabling post-exposure prophylaxis, greatly reduced the risk. New, similar challenges continue to arise, however, from diseases like Ebola.

A truly exceptional example of moral courage occurred on February 28, 2003, when Dr. Carlo Urbani, a 46-year-old Italian physician working with the World Health Organization, diagnosed what is now called the severe acute respiratory distress syndrome (SARS) while working in the Vietnam French Hospital in Hanoi. He chose to stay with the local doctors and nurses who quarantined themselves (to protect their families, the community, and perhaps the rest of the world). At the time, Urbani told his wife, "This will be the end of me." He died of the disease the next month.

Another form of courage is the fortitude to soldier on in the face of rejection or mockery. Joseph Lister's introduction of antisepsis was such an example. His theories, based on Pasteur's work, were initially not accepted in Britain (though they were quickly adopted in Germany). His equanimity in the face of attacks on his experimental work was probably abetted by his Quaker faith, which allowed him to quietly persevere. Sherwin Nuland relates a remark Lister made to one of his residents (later Sir Clair Thomson) after a particularly vigorous sally had been directed against his doctrine by a stubborn colleague. The year was 1863, and the fifty-six-year-old professor had heard just about every argument that could possibly be thrown at him, opposing his system. Wearily and with a quiet certitude, he predicted to his young pupil that the day must surely come when his principles would be universally utilized. Then, casting off his usual soft tone of serenity, Lister raised his voice just a bit to declare with a barely perceptible trace of sternness, "If the profession does not recognize them, the public will learn of them and the law will insist on them."[1]

---

[1] Nuland (1988), 377-8.

Canadian philosopher Douglas Walton[2] defines courage as the overcoming of obstacles to reach a socially desirable goal through the use of moral and practical reasoning. Altruism facilitates moral reasoning; persistence facilitates practical reasoning. Walton offers the following outline:

The Canadian philosopher Douglas Walton views courage as the overcoming of obstacles through the use of both moral reasoning and practical reasoning. Altruism facilitates moral reasoning; persistence facilitates practical reasoning (after Walton 1986).

Lister's example illustrates the model of courage put forth by Walton (Figure above). In his altruism, Lister, following the precepts and discoveries of Pasteur, wanted to eliminate hospital gangrene. Lister's dogged persistence, along with his striking results let him overcome the resistence of some of his peers. (Lister displayed additional courage when he chose to leave his

---

[2] Walton (1986).

professorship at Edinburgh, where he was beloved by students and peers alike, and go to the hostile environment of London to promulgate his theory of antisepsis. Seven hundred students had signed a petition urging him not to leave.)

Another physician, the Polish pediatrician Dr. Janusz Korczak, displayed "the courage unto death." The longtime director of an orphanage in Warsaw, he refused freedom for himself and stayed with the orphans as they were led to the death chambers of a Nazi extermination camp. He died with them.

Osler displayed another type of courage after the death of his son in the First World War, a courage he alluded to as his third ideal when he left the U.S. some thirteen years earlier. That ideal—mentioned in our Preface—was to cultivate **"such a measure of equanimity as would enable me . . . to be ready when the day of sorrow and grief came to meet it with the courage befitting a man."**[3]

Today's changing conditions of medical practice may increasingly require substantial moral courage to stand up for what's best for others, not only for our patients but also for our fellow physicians and other health care workers. We are often caught in a web of conflicting interests, or what ethicists call a "conflict of obligations." Obligations to patients may be discordant with obligations to the health care organization, to third-party payers, and to government regulations. As Drs. Edmund Pellegrino and David Thomasma prophesized:

> To act courageously in . . . an environment of "corporate medicine" will become more and more difficult. There is an increasing demand for physicians who are "team players," people who can function well

---

[3] *L'Envoi.*

in the environment of HMOs and corporate structures. Being a team player does not necessarily preclude acting with courage. Yet it does diminish the likelihood that [we] . . . will speak out courageously about inequities or on behalf of patients when the necessity arises.[4]

We could cite many other examples of courage, including the pressure to give in to "groupthink," as when members of a group place greater value on solidarity, unanimity, and their own self-righteousness than on objective appraisal of the available data. How else can we explain the fierce rivalries bordering on hatred that sometimes erupt between competing physician groups and competing hospitals and health care systems, especially in larger communities? How else can we explain the apparent paucity of *peacemakers* among us? Courage, like the other cardinal virtues, contains many dimensions but its core consists of serving others, of "doing the right thing," despite personal risks.

Playwright George Bernard Shaw put it graphically: "It is courage, courage, courage that raises the blood of life to crimson splendor." More recently, J. K. Rowling's character Albus Dumbledore (headmaster at Hogwarts School) explained to his young charge Harry Potter: "It is our choices, Harry, that show what we really are, far more than our abilities."

As physicians, we should have the COURAGE of our convictions!

---

[4] Pellegrino and Thomasma (1993), 112n.

WISDOM

Courage, humility, and WISDOM are building blocks for character.[1] In that context, what do we mean by wisdom? How does it apply to students of medicine? Aristotle spoke of *phronesis*, by which he meant practical wisdom, the ability to make good decisions in cloudy circumstances. As physicians caring for sick patients, the way is not always certain and we sometimes have to make decisions in unclear situations. In the medical school environment of so many new facts and figures to be mastered, how do we attain wisdom?

First, recognize that wisdom is more than just knowledge. In speaking to the issue of knowledge versus wisdom, Osler mentioned two English poets:

[There] **was a very happy remark of Alfred Lord Tennyson,**[2] **'knowledge grows but wisdom lingers.' After all, the greatest difficulty of life is to make knowledge effective, to convert it into practical wisdom. We often confuse the two, thinking they are identical. But it was another**

---

[1] See section the INFLUENCE OF VIRTUOUS CHARACTER.
[2] Tennyson (1809-1872) succeeded Wordsworth as Poet Laureate of England.

49

poet—Cowper[3]—who said that far from being one, they often have no connection whatsoever.[4]

A third-year medical student who has stuffed her mind with facts in preparation for step 1 of the USMLE process, and who then watches a seasoned clinician reason through a case, will readily appreciate a longer section of Cowper's verse:

> Knowledge and wisdom, far from being one,
> Have ofttimes no connection. Knowledge dwells
> In heads replete with thoughts of other men,
> Wisdom in minds attentive to their own.
> Knowledge, a rude unprofitable mass,
> Till smooth'd and squared and fitted to its place,
> Does but encumber whom it seems to enrich.
> Knowledge is proud that he has learned so much;
> Wisdom is humble that he knows no more.[5]

Regarding gaining wisdom, Osler had this to say:

[For those just starting in practice] **I would like to urge particularly to take careful notes of their cases, and to study each individual patient intelligently. Experience in any disease is not a measure of the number of cases seen; it is not a matter of mere accretion, of the adding fact to fact; [that] is knowledge. True experience brings more than knowledge; it brings wisdom; and this is a question of personal mental development."[6]

---

[3] William Cowper (1731-1800) was a poet and abolitionist. Together with John Newton (1725-1807), the author of "Amazing Grace," Cowper spoke out against slavery.

[4] What the public can do in the fight against tuberculosis.

[5] Cowper W, "The Task, A Poem" (1875).

[6] Osler (1899) On the Study of Pneumonia.

Practical wisdom brings to mind the "Serenity Prayer" of theologian Reinhold Niebuhr: "God grant me the SERENITY to accept the things I cannot change, the COURAGE to change the things I can and the WISDOM to know the difference."

The need for practical wisdom abounds in the practice of medicine and surgery. For example, *phronesis* derived from clinical experience can restrain the seasoned practitioner from being too aggressive. Consider two scenarios, one from medicine (A), and one from surgery (B), in which doctors confront tough decisions. In each, wisdom can lead to a different course of treatment.

(A) An elderly woman with a metastatic malignancy has undergone two courses of aggressive chemotherapy with two new drugs with no evident response. Internist #1 urges a third course—with the almost certain prospect of serious adverse side effects.

Internist #2, after conferring with her and her family, recommends palliative care, in hospice, to let them enjoy her last few weeks together.

(B) An elderly, delirious, frail man presents with an acute, tender abdomen that needs urgent exploration. A plain X-Ray shows an air-filled loop of bowel. Young surgeon #1 suspects a volvulus and assures the patient and family that time is of the essence to fix the problem. He heads straight to the OR. An older, more seasoned surgeon #2, having perceived from speaking with the family that the patient has had a good life and his affairs are in order, takes time to explain there might be a vascular catastrophe. If so, a better course might be to *not* be very aggressive. (The findings turn out to be dead bowel, with most of the small bowel and right colon non-viable from mesenteric thrombosis.)

Surgeon #1 resects from the 4th portion of the duodenum to the transverse colon and does an anastamosis. He leaves the patient with a lethal, short-bowel syndrome, from which—after several weeks (and a course of hyperalimentation costing several thousand dollars)—the man expires.

Surgeon #2 simply closes the abdomen. The surgeon and the nurses keep the patient comfortable. The patient dies in less than 24 hours.

Such decisions are not easy and require practical wisdom and circumspection, considering various options and their costs, and pondering several questions. In today's fast-paced practice of medicine, we often forget to consider the entirety of the patient's life, the "big picture." Too often we employ expensive (and risky) technologies without assessing adequately the life story of the patient and the likely prognosis. Too often we forget to explore the patient's perspectives and values. The framework shown in the Figure below may help medical students and residents as they embark on the difficult task of honing their own decision-making processes.

Try walking through the above clinical scenarios asking the five questions, making use of wisdom criteria developed by Baltes and Smith.[7]

Finally, let's consider how the framework might apply to the tough choices, the forks-in-the-road, that crop up from time to time in our personal lives. Studies suggest that most people endure at least three to five major "crises" over the course of their lives. Decisions made during such crises affect our future happiness and well-being. Perhaps the questions shown in the Figure will help readers of this *vade mecum* resolve a life challenge. To that end we strongly encourage "thinking on paper," making lists of pros and cons for discussion.

---

[7] Baltes and Smith (1990).

Although we can judge whether a decision was "wise" only in retrospect, Baltes and Smith propose that the likelihood of a wise decision depends largely on the quality and quantity of thought (that is, the richness of one's internal debate) in response to the five questions shown here. (After Baltes and Smith)

In 1904 (at age 55) William Osler faced the decision whether to stay in Baltimore or to take a position in Oxford. The Oxford position was prestigious, but the salary would be substantially less and there was no medical school. Indeed, the appointment as Regius Professor of Medicine was to a large extent merely honorific. In the U.S. Osler was famous, useful, and busy too busy. He had tried to limit his private practice, but he found it difficult to say no, especially to doctors and their families who wanted his services. He wrote: **"I am living 'a life of the hunted' at present. Infernal nuisance & yet seems very difficult to limit one's legitimate work."**[8] He had a serious case of what we'd now call "burnout." When he got the offer he was in Eng-

---

[8] Fye (1989).

land. His wife urged him to accept the less-pressured position at Oxford. She cabled: "Do not procrastinate. Better go in a steamer than go in a pine-box."[9] Osler took his wife's advice to his ultimate advantage, reminding us we all do well to listen to the advice of those near and dear!

---

[9] Ibid.

TEMPERANCE

Reflecting on the cardinal virtue TEMPERANCE brings to mind the issue of alcohol, as in the Women's Christian Temperance Union (WCTU), active during Osler's lifetime and dedicated to abstinence. More broadly, temperance (from the Latin *temperentia*) denotes <u>moderation</u> rather than abstinence and references moderation in all things. Temperance as a virtue thus brings to mind Aristotle's Golden Mean. (A classic example: courage is the mean between recklessness and cowardice.)

Observing modern society, intemperate behavior is commonly seen in the pursuit of wealth, possessions, amusement and fame. Being a classical scholar, William Osler couched his warning against excess using classical mythology: **"Who serve the gods die young—Venus, Bacchus, and Vulcan send in no bills in the seventh decade."**[1] By Venus he meant the goddess of love, who **"is heartless"**—think of sexually transmitted disease. By Bacchus he meant the god of wine—more generally of alcohol— who **"hands in heavy bills for payment, in the form of serious disease of the arteries or of the liver, or there is a general breakdown"**—think of cirrhosis or the mortal tariff intoxicated

---

[1] Bean (1968), 187, 188.

drivers exact. By Vulcan he apparently meant smoking; **"Vulcan plays with respectability, he allows a wide margin—unless one is a college man—he sends in his bills late in life"**—think of lung cancer or emphysema. He also said, **"intemperance in the quantity of food taken is almost the rule"**—consider the current epidemic of obesity in our country and its toll. Osler saw the physician as advisor to the patient: **Better than anyone else the physician can say the word in season to the immoral, to the intemperate, to the uncharitable in word and deed."** Osler was temperate in most things, but occasionally smoked.

Concepts advanced by Abraham Maslow,[2] a pioneer of today's humanistic psychology, offer another perspective on temperance. According to Maslow, we have certain basic needs: physical needs, sexual needs, ego needs, esteem needs. Maslow calls these "deficit needs," that must be satisfied before we can progress up the higher rungs of the ladder. The highest plane, which he calls "being needs," consists of self-actualization, namely, "being all you can be." Few people—less than 5% of the population—ever reach the plane of self-actualization. Maslow agreed with the psychiatrist Viktor Frankl[3] that self-actualization occurs in relationship to the people and circumstances around us as a call to service that transcends self-interest. We physicians transcend our own interests to care for those who have entrusted their secrets and their lives to us. We put the interests of our patients above our own.

As regards the temptations of drugs and alcohol for today's doctors, what Osler said to the faculty at McGill holds true for us today:

---

[2] Maslow (1970).
[3] Frankl (1986).

Above all things be strictly temperate. I will not say that you are in duty bound to give up the use of stimulants altogether— though my own convictions on this point are very strong—but this I do say, that the slightest habitual over-indulgence is as the small flaw in some dyke that forms the barrier to a mighty flood, which widening day by day, sooner or later drowns every fair promise and brings inevitable ruin.[4]

William Osler with his first residents at the Johns Hopkins Hospital. The "house staff" were just that—they lived in the hospital (or "house").

---

[4] Osler (1874-75).

Osler subscribed to what we might call a "heroic" model of medicine whereby the physician makes enormous sacrifices to do his or her best at caring for others. But in his day, his residents literally lived in the hospital, most were not married, and women comprised a small percent of each class. Matters are quite different today.

Debt is a significant problem for many of today's graduating medical students. (Tuition when the authors of this *vade mecum* were students was much less.) The average debt for some graduating seniors is over $100,000, and for some students that debt becomes a factor in selecting a specialty. Few graduates today are debt-free.[5] In some cases students have decided to join the military during their training to lessen the burden of finances, to serve up to twenty years as pay-back, and to then enter private practice as a second career. (See the section on **Finance** in the chapter The Balanced Life.)

How much money do you need to make? It's logical to think that more money buys more happiness. However, data suggest that beyond an income of, say, about $130,000 a year (in 2016 dollars), additional money buys very little additional happiness.[6] Beyond a certain comfort level happiness thus depends largely on things money can't buy such as health, family and friends, outside interests, spiritual enrichment, and the satisfaction that comes from serving others. Likewise, happiness depends less and less on financial statements, high-priced possessions, and lavish lifestyles. All senior physicians know colleagues who've amassed small fortunes only to find their personal lives in shambles.

What, then, can we recommend about the virtue of temperance for physicians in training? Here are four brief suggestions:

---

[5] Ludmerer (2015).

[6] Bok (1993).

- Value the simple and temperate life. Pay off any student loans and other deficits accrued during the long years of training, and then set reasonable limits on deficit needs. Remember why you chose medicine in the first place: to serve others.
- Use temperance to facilitate your search for the proper mean between behavioral extremes. Pay attention, for example, to how you balance technical engrossment with empathic concern for the patient. Pay attention to how you balance diagnostic and therapeutic aggressiveness with caution (or, in the language of bioethics, how you balance the principles of beneficence and non-maleficence).
- When pondering cost vs. benefit, consider not just fiscal costs, but also the cost in suffering to your patient of decisions you make, and the tests and studies you order.
- Help your fellow citizens set reasonable limits on utilization of medical resources. It's been said that Americans are "addicted to addiction." Perhaps, just perhaps, it may be possible for the younger generations of physicians to facilitate a national dialogue on the limits of medicine and the appropriate goals of health care.

JUSTICE

What is JUSTICE? In a word, it is <u>Fairness</u>. When U.S. citizens recite the Pledge of Allegiance they subscribe to the democratic concept of "liberty and justice for all." It sounds good in the pledge, but anyone familiar with American history knows the pursuit of justice has been far from simple.

Seeking justice is important for physicians. It is one of the four classic cardinal virtues (along with wisdom, temperance and courage), and is also one of the four principles of medical ethics (along with beneficence, nonmaleficence and autonomy) put forth by Beauchamp and Childress.[1]

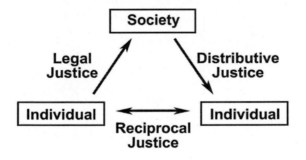

---

[1] Beauchamp and Childress (2012).

Pieper[2] outlines three forms of justice that can be applied to medical practice (Figure). At the base is reciprocal justice, which traditionally has embraced all that we call the doctor-patient relationship. (Although a plethora of third parties—insurance companies and government—have intervened.) What was straightforward in the practice of our physician grandfathers has become quite complex today.

A second category (legal justice) embraces the rules, regulations and legal remedies that apply to medical practice. (Doctors should be familiar with their own states' medical practice act.) We should here say a brief word about legal justice as it bears on the physician's role as expert witness. Most medical malpractice cases are based on *a theory of negligence* in which the plaintiff must establish that the treating physician deviated from an applicable *standard of care*. Unfortunately, some physicians in the U.S. regularly pad their incomes by serving as "professional" expert witnesses willing to give testimony strongly biased toward the side that is paying them. Since physician expert witnesses are essential to malpractice litigation, serving in this capacity— whether for plaintiff or defense—should be undertaken with the highest sense of ethics, professionalism, intellectual honesty, and genuine empathy for all parties: the patient, the patient's significant others, and the physicians who stand accused of negligence.

I (JBV) recall a situation in which I was asked to review a case (a colon injury during laparoscopic cholecystectomy) that caused an expensive complication (an intra-abdominal abscess), in which the defending surgeon strongly did not wish to settle the case. Review of a video done during the operation showed the operator vigorously cauterizing (really *frying!*) a bleeder he

---

[2] Pieper (1966).

thought was in the mesentery—that was actually on the wall of the colon—which led to the colon perforation and the abscess. I recommended the insurance company settle the case. The surgeon was resistant and wanted to "deep-six" (*i.e.* destroy) the tape— tantamount to changing the record. That would have been very serious, had it been discovered, and might have even resulted in punitive damages. The case was settled.

The third type (distributive justice)—applying as it does to society's obligations to its individual members—is by far the most problematic, divisive, and challenging, dividing as it does people into liberals, conservatives, libertarians, and so forth. Here are two examples.

Consider the 1993 case of a double transplant for Pennsylvania Governor Robert P. Casey,[3] whose heart and liver were failing due to amyloidosis. He had previously had a quadruple coronary bypass. At the time the waiting list time for a liver transplant was 67 days, for a heart transplant 198 days. Yet within *13 hours* the doctors in Pittsburgh located donor organs of the right size, tissue type, and blood type for him. "We were concerned about people's perception this smacks of favoritism or conspiracy," Dr. John Fung, one of the surgeons later said. Casey did well, served out his (second) term as governor and lived another seven years, dying in 2000 at age 68. Was this fair? Is one person's life more valuable than another? Are there mitigating circumstances in such cases?

(It reminded us of an exchange between a king and a surgeon:

KING: "I hope you will care for the King better than the poor."

---

[3] www.bloomberg.com/news/articles/1993-06-27/governor-caseys-timely-transplant

SURGEON: "No, Sire, that is impossible."

KING: "Why so?"

SURGEON: "Because I care for them as much as I do for kings."

The King was Charles IX, the surgeon was Ambroise Paré, the country was France and the time was the late sixteenth century.[4])

A second case is the famous 2005 case of Terri Schiavo[5], about a woman who had been in a persistent vegetative state for 15 years following a cardiac arrest, which ultimately reached the U.S. Congress and the President. The Schiavo case illustrated problems of (1) reciprocal justice between doctors and their patients; (2) legal accountability of physicians to statutory law and judicial decisions; and (3) the appropriateness of expending large amounts of societal resources for the care of one individual with a severely limited prognosis.

All physicians should recognize *social responsibility* as a crucial aspect of justice. Most American physicians endorse community participation, political involvement, and collective advocacy, and indeed a survey suggested that about two-thirds of doctors had participated in at least one of these three categories during the previous three years.[6] As medicine becomes increasingly population-based, as disparities in health care continue to widen; as the American public debates whether health care should be a "right" and, if so, to what extent; and as new threats to human survival continue to emerge, civic-minded physicians will find new opportunities to promote the public interest and, in so doing, reassert the place of medicine among

---

[4] *The Oslerian* [newsletter of the American Osler Society] 2016; 17(2): 1-3.

[5] https://en.wikipedia.org/wiki/Terri_Schiavo_case

[6] Gruen et al (2006).

the world's noblest humanitarian professions. Unfortunately, most of today's graduating students will enter practice with substantial debts that may preclude heavy involvement in social causes, at least for a while. We recommend that students and young physicians should *think* about how they might best serve society and, when the time is right, stand up for their convictions. Osler thus told students: Students and young physicians should explore the possibilities for such service: **"And, if the fight is for principle and justice, even when failure seems certain, where many have failed before, cling to your ideal . . ."**[7]

---

[7] Aequanimitas.

FAITH

The terms "faith" and "belief" both express confidence, trust, or acceptance of something that cannot be proved beyond all doubt. However, there is a growing sense that "faith" is more nuanced than "belief." We like others suggest that "faith" should be recognized as an *active verb* in English, as it is in Hebrew and Latin. As an active verb, "faith" would mean "*moving toward*" confidence, trust, or acceptance of something that cannot be proved beyond all doubt. Faith thus opposes "doubt," which denotes "*moving away from*" such confidence, trust, and acceptance, as illustrated in the Figure.

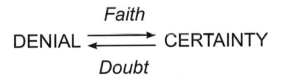

"Faith" as an active verb denotes the process of moving toward confidence and trust in a proposition that cannot be proved with absolute certainty, just as "doubt" denotes the process of moving toward denial.

A mature spiritual life, we like to believe, uses the active verbs "faith" and "doubt" to negotiate the tension between "certainty" and "denial," a tension that applies to most of what we do as doctors.

We "faith" that our plan of care is best for a patient despite occasional reservations about it. We do our best while recalling the apocryphal words of the medical school dean who told a graduating class, "Half of what we've taught you is wrong—the problem is, we don't know which half!" And, just as we "faith" what's best for the patient, the patient must "faith" in us!

Osler used "faith" often and it's our sense that he would have endorsed using "faith" as a verb. He opined that **"such as we find it, faith is a most precious commodity, without which we should be very badly off."**[1] He additionally declared: **"Nothing in life is more wonderful than faith—the one great moving force which we can neither weigh in the balance nor test in the crucible. Intangible as the ether, ineluctable as gravitation, the radium of the moral and mental spheres, indefinable, known only by its effects, faith pours out an unfailing stream of energy . . ."**[2] In preparing the seventh edition of *The Principles and Practice of Medicine* he was encouraged to write about the importance of "faith" in doctors or in remedies, to describe what we now call the placebo effect. He thus wrote:

> **In all ages, and in all lands, the prayer of faith, to use the words of St. James, has healed the sick; and we must remember that amid the Æsculapian cult, the most elaborate and beautiful system of faith-healing the world has seen, scientific medicine took its rise. As a profession, consciously or unconsciously, more often the latter, *faith* has been one of our most**

---

[1] Medicine in the nineteenth century.
[2] The faith that heals.

valuable assets, and Galen expressed a great truth when he said, "He cures most successfully in whom the people have the greatest confidence."[3]

On the other hand, **"A man must have faith in himself to be of any use in the world. There may be very little on which to base it—no matter, but faith in one's powers, in one's mission is essential to success. Confidence once won, the rest follows naturally; and with a strong faith in himself a man becomes a local center for its radiation."**[4]

But we think of "faith" most commonly in the domain of religion, and it's here—"faith" as applied to the Big Questions of our existence—that we encounter difficulties. In that regard, believers in all the major religions (as well as agnostics and atheists) manifest "faith" in universal moral precepts.

Religious anxiety markedly characterized the Victorian era (1837-1901) during which Osler came of age. As the son of an Anglican priest, he was immersed in the Bible from early childhood and cherished its stories and traditions the rest of his life. Yet in 1859, when he was but ten years of age, Charles Darwin's publication of *The Origin of the Species* shook the foundations of Christianity. Scholars using the tools of philology (literary criticism, historical analysis, and linguistics) joined the attack on the inerrancy of scripture. To Osler's rescue came his first copy of *Religio Medici*[5] by Sir Thomas Browne (see page 150). The *Religio,* which had made its 37-year-old author famous overnight, first appeared as an unauthorized version in 1642, the year the English Civil War erupted over disputes freighted with differences over religious beliefs and practices.

---

[3] Cushing (1925), ii, 181-2.

[4] The faith that heals.

[5] *Religio Medici*, Part 1, section 6.

Browne's *Religio* does not provide a coherent theology; as a professor of English recently wrote: "Browne's version of the harmonious coexistence of faith and reason is not a marriage, but a divorce settlement: each faculty gets custody of the issues proper to it—and so long as each stays out of the other's way, all is well."[6] However, the *Religio* as an expression of faith is perhaps best read as a psychological autobiography of one man's continuous negotiation of the rocky terrain between denial and certainty. Having carefully read Browne's *Religio*, CSB offers the following take-home points from Browne, that remain worthy of consideration, some 370 years later:

- Religious truth (or "belief system") is a highly individual matter.
- It is wise to tolerate differences of opinion about religious truth. We should be respectful of patients' beliefs.
- It is never a good idea to go to war over disputes about religion.
- Worship (religious practice; "following the great wheel of the church") can be useful for the individual even if he or she entertains doubts about "truth."
- "Faith" is best seen as a process, a journey rather than a final destination, since our opinions concerning "truth" vary over time.

Osler recognized in Sir Thomas Browne a kindred spirit and one who, despite whatever reservations he might have had concerning "truth," never gave up on "faith" in its larger sense. Osler told students **"One and all of you will have to face the ordeal of every student in this generation who sooner or later**

---

[6] Conti (2008).

tries to mix the waters of science with the oil of faith. You can have a great deal of both if you only keep them separate."[7] One thinks of another venerated scientist, Louis Pasteur (a Catholic) who described how he kept science and religion separate in his own life, saying "When I go into my laboratory I put on my white coat; when I step out, I take it off."[8]

When Osler gave the Ingersoll Lecture at Harvard in 1904,[9] he divided believers into three groups as concerned their belief in immortality. (It's interesting to consider see how well these groups still apply to people today!):

- The *Laodiceans*, who like the lukewarm early Christians of Laodicea, professed belief in immortality but did not allow it to influence their lives. They were **"concerned less with the future life than with the price of beef . . ."**
- The *Gallioneans*, who, like such Roman officials as the aloof Junio Gallio, were unconcerned about the issue of immortality. They were agnostics, who **"have either reached the intellectual conviction that there is no hope in the grave, or the question remains open"** and are therefore satisfied with **"the absorbing interest of other problems."**
- The *Teresians*, who, like the nuns and friars who followed St. Teresa, took religious faith as the controlling force in their lives. Osler found these people—**"true believers"** as we would now call them—to be the most interesting.

---

[7] The master-word in medicine.
[8] Vallery-Radot (1924).
[9] *Science and Immortality.*

Osler asserted that **"the scientific student should be ready to acknowledge the value of a belief in a hereafter as an asset to human life."** He continued: **"The man of science is in a sad quandary today. He cannot but feel that the emotional side to which faith leans makes for all that is bright and joyous in life. Fed on the dry husks of facts, the human heart has a hidden want which science cannot supply . . ."** He advised: **"To keep his mind sweet the modern scientific man should be saturated with the Bible and Plato, with Homer, Shakespeare, and Milton; to see life through their eyes may enable him to strike a balance between the rational and the emotional, which is the most serious difficulty of the intellectual life."** And he then let loose a summation of his perspective on the subject of immortality:

> **A word in conclusion to the young men in the audience. As perplexity of soul will be your lot and portion, accept the situation with a good grace. The hopes and fears which make us men are inseparable, and this wine-press of Doubt each of you must tread alone. It is a trouble from which no man may deliver his brother or make agreement with another for him. . . . On the question before us wide and far your hearts will range from those early days. . . . In certain of you the changes and chances of the years ahead will reduce this to a vague sense of eternal continuity. . . . In a very few it will be begotten again as the lively hope of the Teresians; while a majority will retain the sabbatical interest of the Laodiceans. . . . Some of you will wander through all phases, to come at last, I trust, to the opinion of Cicero, who had rather be mistaken with Plato** [who believed in the immortality of the soul]

than be right with those who deny altogether the life after death; and this is my own *confessio fidei*.[10]

Modern medical students can "keep their mind sweet" by regular reading in their bedside library (see Appendix C).

---

[10] *Science and Immortality.*

HOPE

HOPE among the transcendent virtues (Faith, Hope and Love) is relevant to students and residents in three ways: In the everyday care of patients; in end-of-life situations, and in the physician's own life-management strategies.

The encounter between patient and doctor is suffused with hope. Most patients come to us with the hope of relief for their suffering. By our demeanor and deportment we can build on that hope. Osler wrote: **"Once gain the confidence of a patient and inspire him with hope, and the battle is half won."**[1] He echoed Galen: **"As Galen says, confidence and hope do more good than physic [medication]—'he cures most in whom most are confident.'"**[2]

Hope likewise goes hand-in-hand with cheerfulness. Osler is often quoted to the effect that one should always leave the bedside (or the clinic examining room) with a cheerful expression projecting hope and optimism.

In Osler's day—before antibiotics or chemotherapy or joint replacement for orthopedic problems—almost all care was palliative. Consider this statement by Harvard physiologist Lawrence J. Henderson: "Sometime between 1910 and 1912 in

---

[1] The reserves of life.
[2] Medicine in the nineteenth century.

this country, a random patient, with a random disease, consulting a doctor chosen at random had, for the first time in the history of mankind, a better than fifty-fifty chance of profiting from the encounter."[3] Today we have much better odds, but we still need to preserve and encourage hope.

As relates diagnoses of cancer or other ominous diseases, in Osler's day, and even up to the time we (CSB and JBV) were in school, most patients were NOT informed about a dismal prognosis unless they asked. Today the trend is toward full disclosure, but the manner in which a poor prognosis is conveyed—***how*** we impart it—is crucial to the preservation of hope. It is unkind and often counterproductive to be bluntly frank in conveying bad news. Consider the following exchange related by Norman Cousins in his book *Head First: The Biology of Hope*:[4]

> A California physician told me about the emotional devastation experienced by his son, seventeen, following surgery for cancer. The day following the operation the surgeon came into the recovery room and, in the presence of the patient, told the father that he should expect the death of his son in a matter of days, perhaps a week at most.
>
> The father was shocked not just by the catastrophic news but by the fact that the surgeon had no hesitation in delivering the verdict in the presence of the patient.
>
> "I followed the surgeon out of the room," he told me, "and as a fellow physician, berated him for his reprehensible conduct. He seemed surprised by my

---

[3] Strauss (1968), 302.

[4] Cousins (1989), 100.

anger and defended himself by saying that doctors had to be honest and that patients should not be deceived. He missed the point. He should have consulted with me first and we could have decided on what ought to be done or said under the circumstances.

"I came back into the room and told my son that I had just chewed out the surgeon and that I had known too many patients who made surprising comebacks to justify the kind of verdict the surgeon delivered. I told my son to disregard what the surgeon said and we would work together in proving him wrong. My son believed me. He sailed through the first week after the surgery and has been in remission ever since. That was four years ago and my son is living a normal life in every way.

"I suppose doctors feel they are only doing their duty when they level with patients," he continued, "and most of the time their predictions are correct. But even if they are wrong only ten percent of the time, they're taking an awful chance of hurting a patient. Anyway, I thought the surgeon went out of his way to hang black crepe over my son."

Here is Osler regarding such a situation: **"What is your duty in the matter of telling a patient that he is probably the subject of an incurable disease? . . . One thing is certain; it is not for you to don the black cap, and, assuming the judicial function, take away hope from any patient—'hope that comes to all.'"**[5] Likewise he advised (and in doing so perhaps anticipated the idea of palliative care):

---

[5] Osler W (1897) Lectures on Angina Pectoris and Allied States, 142.

"A disease may be incurable and the best we can do is to relieve symptoms and to make the patient comfortable. . . . It is a hard matter and really not often necessary (since nature usually does it quietly and in good time) to tell a patient that he is past all hope. As Sir Thomas Browne says: 'It is the hardest stone you can throw at a man to tell him that he is at the end of his tether;' and yet, put in the right way to an intelligent man it is not always cruel."[6]

Finally, hope plays a role in managing our personal lives, especially in dealing with setbacks. Setbacks should serve as triggers to reflect and reevaluate our goals. Seek hope as an Aristotelian mean between *despair* (unwarranted pessimism) and Pollyannaish *presumption* (unwarranted optimism). Then set new goals.

For physicians, a common setback is when a patient dies under our care, despite our best efforts. Hope means, on the one hand, that we do not respond with rage or despair, nor on the other hand, do we merely shrug off what happened. In such situations it is helpful to discuss it with a trusted friend or colleague. In that regard, a good change that's occurred since the authors were in training is the effort to take a debriefing "time out" to respond and reflect in such situations rather than "stuff" or suppress our emotions.[7] Hope lets us heal and move on

Here are some suggestions regarding hope:

- Be upbeat and cheerful in your encounters with patients. Recall the wisdom of the proverb, "A cheerful heart is good medicine."[8]

---

[6] The treatment of disease.

[7] Mullan PC et al (2014).

[8] Proverbs 17:22.

- In conveying a guarded prognosis, do not quench hope. Be honest but not blunt or cruel. Reaffirm that you (and your patient) are together and you will be with them, come what may. Always bear in mind the fears patients have about the future, about the unknown, and reassure them that you will be there for them. For many sick patients, a great fear is abandonment, so continue making rounds and visit your patients each day, despite a grim prognosis. Recall Trudeau's maxim: To cure sometimes, to relieve often, to comfort always.[9]

- Habitually apply hope to setbacks in your own life, taking time to review and re-evaluate and learn from the experience.

---

[9] Strauss (1968), 410a. This maxim is inscribed at the base of a statue of Edward Livingston Trudeau sculpted by Gutzon Borglum in Saranac Lake, NY. The saying has been variously attributed to Trudeau (1848-1915), to Ambroise Paré (1510-1590), and even to Hippocrates (c.460-370 BC).

LOVE

L OVE reigns supreme among the transcendent virtues and is foundational to the world's great religions. St. Paul crowned love the highest of the transcendent virtues (1 Corinthians 13:13) and thus it has remained in Christianity. The Jewish sage Hillel, the Elder, a contemporary of Jesus of Nazareth and who like Jesus insisted that love matters more than the law, was once challenged to recite the entire Torah while standing on one foot. He replied in effect: "Love the Lord with all your heart and love your neighbor as yourself. That is the entire Torah. All the rest is commentary." And one of Osler's favorite poems was "Abou Ben Adhem," by the English poet Leigh Hunt (1784-1859), inspired by the semi-historical story of one of the most celebrated early saints of Islam, Ibrahim ibn Adhem (c718-c782). Hunt's poem, important to Osler as an expression of humanism, can form part of any physician's credo, his or her religious beliefs and practices. (We reproduce it at the end of this section.)

Osler was a beloved physician. Lewellys Barker, who came down from Toronto to serve as a resident under Osler and became his successor at Johns Hopkins, knew him well. He wrote about "the Chief":

> "Through native capacity and wide professional and social experience Dr. Osler had acquired an unusual

knowledge of human nature; his intuitions of the character and personality for those with whom he came in contact were almost uncanny. One was reminded of the fine saying of Leonardo da Vinci: "True and great love springs out of great knowledge, and where you know little you can love but little or not at all." He won friendship and affection because he loved his fellow man and because of his recognition of the best qualities in, and of the good intentions, of the men and women about him. He never permitted himself to judge a human being adversely, and he had an unusual power of putting himself by imagination fully in his fellow's place."[1]

LOVE as the supreme transcendent virtue is not easy to define, at least in English. The philosopher Josef Pieper asked: "Does the noun 'love' cover a single, or approximately single, area of meaning—or is it not rather something like an archipelago of extremely varied meanings with no discernible connections among them?"[2] The ancient Greeks spoke of three kinds of love—*philia, agape,* and *eros*—which for our purposes as physicians gives us a convenient way to discuss LOVE as it relates to our colleagues, our patients, and those with whom we share our lives.

Philia commonly denotes "brotherly [or sisterly] love," the kind of love we should display toward our colleagues in the health professions. Here the Latin term for love (*caritas*) translated as charity in the King James Version of the Bible is meaningful. Hear Osler on this kind of love: "**The law of the higher life**

[1] Barker L (1926), 243.

[2] Pieper J (1997), 145.

is only fulfilled by love, i.e. charity. . . . Show in your daily life tenderness and consideration to the weak, infinite pity to the suffering, and broad charity to all."[3] Osler advised charity and equanimity in our approach to those with whom we live and work: **"One of the first essentials in securing a good-natured equanimity is not to expect too much of the people amongst whom you dwell. . . . Deal gently then with this deliciously credulous old human nature in which we work, and restrain your indignation."**[4]

As in all of life, you'll find it easy to love the loveable patient, but a bit challenging to love the indifferent, ungrateful, or even hateful patient, not to mention the patient who fails to comply with recommendations, or who repeatedly returns to the hospital or clinic with behavioral or substance-abuse issues. As your career progresses, you'll also find it easy to love your fellow health care workers who are lovable and easy to work with, but a challenge to love those who are indifferent, rude, or demanding. You may also find it difficult to love hard-nosed administrators, government regulators, and plaintiff attorneys who cross your path. Mark this well: Love goes hand in-hand with charity toward your neighbor.

Dr. George Harrell (1908-1999), founding dean at two medical schools and a past president of AOS, did not know Osler personally. But after reviewing what Osler's contemporaries had to say he concluded: "The veneration in which Osler was held by his students, house officers, colleagues, and patients was due to an uncanny ability to make each individual feel at the moment he or she was the only one who mattered, even though he might be in a crowd around a bed or at a meeting."[5] That sort of love is highly

---

[3] The master-word in medicine.

[4] Aequanimitas.

[5] Harrell (1985).

personal and focused. It does not allow for the multitasking we see so prevalent in our electronically driven society! That love as it relates to our patients is inextricably bound to our service to them. Consider the words of Dr. Albert Schweitzer (1875-1965)[6] as they relate to service, love, and happiness: "I don't know what your destiny will be, but one thing I know. The only ones among you who will really be happy are those who have sought and found how to serve. . . . Success is not the key to happiness. Happiness is the key to success. If you love what you are doing you will be successful."

As observers of life, we physicians are privileged to see love as manifest in our patients. Through the years various philosophers and psychologists have suggested that pure *agape* love is rare, but in our professional lives, we encounter it surprisingly often, and worthy of mention. Few things in medicine are more moving than the sight of a devoted spouse caring for a partner suffering from chronic, severely-debilitating neurologic disease. We see there an *agape* love for the severely-impaired partner, an existential love, a love with no hope for reciprocation.

We assume most readers of this *vade mecum* hold out the hope for a lifelong partner, and it is the *eros* love in our closest relationships—with whom we share our lives—that can support and sustain us; it is the haven where we can seek shelter. There is wisdom and comfort in the words of explorer Richard E. Byrd (1888-1957), who spent months alone in Antarctica:[7] "In the end, only two things matter to a [person], regardless of who he [or she] is, and they are the affection and understanding of a family . . . the family is an everlasting anchorage, a quiet harbor where [our] ships can be left to swing in the moorings of pride and loyalty."

---

[6] Schweitzer (1935).
[7] Byrd (1938).

While Osler's religious life has been the subject of much speculation, there is a consensus that he sought meaning mainly through his work, his overflowing love of humanity, his deep interest in the humanities, and his reverence for the great figures of the past and present who contributed to the welfare of humankind. Hence, as AOS member Gary Ferngren writes, Osler remains "a model of medical humanism in a world in which medicine . . . [is] increasingly dominated by science and technology."[8] Osler's humanistic counsel appealed to a wide variety of persons, and he never declared himself as being a member of a specific denomination. Biographer Michael Bliss[9] indicates that Osler would never discuss issues of religious belief, and instead hid behind a response he had read about:

"What is your religion, sir?"
"Mine is the religion of all sensible men."
"And pray, what is that?"
"Why all sensible men keep religion to themselves."

"Abou Ben Adhem"
by Leigh Hunt[10]

Abou Ben Adhem (may his tribe increase!)
Awoke one night from a deep dream of peace,
And saw, within the moonlight in his room,
Making it rich, and like a lily in bloom,
An angel writing in a book of gold:—

---

[8] Ferngren (2000).
[9] Bliss M (1999), 291.
[10] From https://www.poetryfoundation.org/poems-and-poets/poems/detail/44433

Exceeding peace had made Ben Adhem bold,
And to the presence in the room he said,
"What writest thou?" The vision raised its head,
And with a look made of all sweet accord,
Answered, "The names of those who love the Lord."
"And is mine one?" said Abou. "Nay, not so,"
Replied the angel. Abou spoke more low,
But cheerly still; and said, "I pray thee, then,
Write me as one that loves his fellow men."
The angel wrote, and vanished. The next night
It came again with a great wakening light,
And showed the names whom love of God had blest,
And lo! Ben Adhem's name led all the rest.

THE BALANCED LIFE

DAY-TIGHT COMPARTMENTS

Osler's first personal ideal was **"to do the day's work well and not to bother about to-morrow."** He stated that to this ideal, **"more than anything else, I owe whatever success I have had—to this power of settling down to the day's work and trying to do it well to the best of one's ability, and letting the future take care of itself."**[1] This simple idea was famously expressed in 23 B.C. by the Roman poet Horace as *carpe diem*, usually translated "seize the day," but also translatable as "use," "make use of," or "enjoy" the day. The message is simple: To ruminate about the past or fret about the future limits our effectiveness in the here-and-now. How easily we forget this truism!

Most readers will identify with Osler's predicament when, while studying for an exam at age 22, he couldn't concentrate because of doubts about his future. Was medicine the right choice? Should he be studying to be a minister instead? Or should he go into business, like his older brother Edmund Boyd Osler ("E.B.," who became one of Canada's wealthiest citizens"), or go into law, like his brother Britton Bath Osler ("B.B.," who was

---

[1] L'envoi.

a leading trial lawyer) or his brother Featherston (who became a distinguished jurist)? Osler got up from his chair and pulled from a shelf a volume by Thomas Carlyle, the nineteenth-century Scottish historian, philosopher, and ethicist. Turning to a random page he found a passage that read, "Our main business is not to see what lies dimly in the distance but to do what lies clearly at hand." As Osler later put it: **"A commonplace sentiment enough, but it hit, and stuck, and helped, and was the starting point of a habit that has enabled me to utilize to the full, the single talent entrusted to me."**[2] It changed his life, as he later told medical students:

> **"I started in life—I may as well own up and admit—with just an ordinary everyday stock of brains. In my schooldays I was much more bent upon mischief than upon books—I say it with regret now—but as soon as I got interested in medicine I had only a single idea and I do believe that if I have had any measure of success at all, it has been solely because of doing the day's work well that was before me just as faithfully and honestly and energetically as was in my power."**[3]

Osler drew his metaphor of "day-tight compartments" from the watertight compartments of the great ocean liners of his era. As he explained to Yale students in a lecture entitled "A Way of Life":

> **I stood on the bridge of one of the great liners, ploughing the ocean at 25 knots. "She is alive," said**

---

[2] Fulton (1949).
[3] Cushing (1925), i, 81.

my companion, "in every plate; a huge monster with brain and nerves, an immense stomach, a wonderful heart and lungs, and a splendid system of locomotion." Just at that moment a signal sounded and all over the ship the watertight compartments were closed. "Our chief factor of safety," said the Captain. "In spite of the *Titanic*," I said. "Yes," he replied, "in spite of the *Titanic*." Now each of you is a much more marvelous organization than the great liner, and bound on a longer voyage. What I urge is that you learn to control the machinery as to live with "day-tight compartments" as the most certain way to ensure safety on the voyage. Get to the bridge, and see that at least the great bulkheads are in working order. Touch a button and hear, at every level of your life, the iron doors shutting out the Past—the dead yesterdays. Touch another and shut off, with a metal curtain, the Future—the unborn to-morrows. Then you are safe—safe for to-day![4]

Osler hammered this point home: "Shut off the past! Let the dead past bury its dead. So easy to say, so hard to realize! The truth is, the past haunts us like a shadow. To disregard it is not easy."[5] Moreover, he asserted:

The load of to-morrow, added to that of yesterday, carried to-day makes the strongest falter. Shut off the future as tightly as the past. No dreams, no visions, no delicious fantasies, no castles in the air, with which, as the old song so truly says, "hearts are broken, heads

---

[4] A Way of Life.
[5] Ibid.

are turned." To youth, we are told, belongs the future, but the wretched to-morrow that so plagues some of us has no certainty, except through to-day. Who can tell us what a day may bring forth? . . . The future is to-day—there is no to-morrow! The day of a man's salvation is *now*—the life of the present, of to-day, lived earnestly, intently, without a forward-looking thought, is the only insurance for the future. Let the limit of your horizon be a twenty-four-hour circle.[6]

Olser's accent on day-tight compartments has been re-asserted today by the emphasis placed on the practice of *mindfulness*, of us each being aware of the here and now. Swiss Psychiatrist Christophe Andre's 2015 book[7] is an excellent monograph devoted to that topic through the medium of art.

A senior medical student (at Rutgers)[8] who reviewed this manuscript made this comment: "The Day-tight compartments chapter seems to basically suggest—always stay in the present. One of the strategies I have employed that has been very successful in helping me achieve this consistently is meditating/breathing exercises. Ten minutes in the morning will allow me to close the door on the past and shut the blinds of the future, and allow me to focus on the present." Sylvester cited a link to a *New York Times* article from 2009: (http://www.nytimes.com/2016/11/09/well/mind/breathe-exhale-repeat-the-benefits-of-controlled-breathing.html?_r=0)

Contemporaries marveled at Osler's use of time. His philosophy of "day-tight compartments" underscored the importance of control of the mind, or "being in the moment":

---

[6] Ibid.

[7] Andre C (2015) *Looking at Mindfulness.*

[8] Personal communication 14 November 2016 from Michael John Sylvester.

"Control of the mind as a working machine, the adaptation in it of habit, so that its action becomes almost as automatic as walking, is the end of education—and yet how rarely reached! It can be accomplished with deliberation and repose, never with hurry and worry. Realize how much time there is, how long the day is. Realize that you have sixteen waking hours, three or four of which at least should be devoted to making silent conquest of your mental machinery."[9] And: **"Let each hour of the day have its allotted duty, and cultivate that power of concentration which grows with its exercise, so that the attention neither flags nor wavers, but settles with a bull-dog tenacity on the subject before you."**[10]

Osler became adept at handling interruptions. He became skilled at protecting time for things he really wanted to do such as reviewing the newest journals in the library. He learned to artfully manage people inclined to waste his time: **"Save the fleeting minute; do not stop by the way. Learn gracefully to dodge the bore. Strike first and quickly, and before he has recovered from the blow, be gone; 'tis the only way."**[11]

Osler's simple philosophy of "day-tight compartments" is not without critics, one of whom considered it "for the oarsmen of society; for followers rather than leaders; for carry-outers rather than deciders-orderers."[12] This criticism is well-taken, for a philosophy of "day-tight compartments" makes sense only if

---

[9] A Way of Life.
[10] The master-word in medicine.
[11] Thayer (1931).
[12] Redelmeier (2005).

one sets aside time for setting goals—short term, longer term, and perhaps life-long goals. "Time management"[13] as a serious topic for books, seminars, and the like was rudimentary in Osler's day, if it existed at all. A life spent in "day-tight compartments" makes sense only if one sets aside time to review the past and contemplate the future.

Here's a mini-course in time management that CSB gives to all young people willing to listen:

- Buy an inexpensive notebook. (Spend no more than one dollar on it.)
- Go to a private place—for example a back booth in a fast-food restaurant in a part of town where people are unlikely to recognize you.
- Spend at least 30 minutes thinking and writing down your thoughts.
- Write out your "unifying principles" that you are unwilling to compromise—simple things, such as "live as though seen" and "be as honest as the day is long." Principles set in writing, like the fur liner in an overcoat, will help you weather many temptations through the years.
- Dream.
- Then, write down some long-term goals in all the major areas of life (see the next section, "The Balanced Life").
- Write out your intermediate goals (say, one-year and five-year).
- Put the notebook in the back of a drawer, and don't show it to anybody—not even your significant other.
- Review the notebook at a regular time each week—let's say, at 8:30 each Sunday evening. Briefly review your

---

[13] Inlow (1964).

principles and goals, and then write out your goals for the coming week.
- Each evening, write out your plans (schedule) for the following day. Prioritize the things you'd like to get done over and above your obligatory daily schedule. This may help you sleep better, since worrying about whether you'll forget to do something tomorrow contributes to insomnia.

A body of evidence supports the idea that people who are goal-setters—people who plan—obtain a disproportionate share of the good things life has to offer. But perhaps the greatest benefit of regular goal-setting is the relief of anxiety. You can tell yourself, for example, that "I'm not going to worry about my long-term plans right now, since I'll look at these at 8:30 on Sunday night." Again—try it!

THE BALANCED LIFE

When the authors of this *vade mecum* were in training, we put in long hours—averaging over 100 hours per week—and in retrospect, we led unbalanced lives. True, we were following what Osler called "the Master-word in medicine"[1]—the secret of success—which was **work**, but it exacted a toll, and we believe balance is important in life. Following the design below, balance is worth discussing as one embarks on a career in medicine.

Ideally, one should have written goals in all the major areas of life, developed around a "major definite purpose." This is more difficult than it looks!

---

[1] The master-word in medicine.

Significant changes have occurred since Osler's day: house officers do not live in the hospital, most are married and many have families, and today half the students in a medical school class are women. While Osler, we believe, would have defined as his major definite purpose to become a great teacher of medicine (which he certainly achieved) students or residents today probably would list their major definite purpose as becoming a caring physician while leading a balanced life. Proceeding around the circle (which lists the segments alphabetically), we offer some thoughts.

The vertical spoke of **Habits** highlights the importance of *habitual behavior,* a key factor in any physician's life, as Osler recognized: **"How can you take the greatest possible advantage of your capacities with the least possible strain? By cultivating system. I say cultivating advisedly, since some of you will find the acquisition of systematic habits very hard."**[2] In brief, Osler meant being organized and disciplined, careful about time management. In his book *Seven Habits of Highly Effective People,*[3] author Steven Covey lists seven habits that are as effectual today as they were when he wrote the book in 1989: (1) Be proactive; (2) Be imaginative; (3) Put first things first; (4) Think win-win; (5) Seek first to understand, then to be understood; (6) Synergize—encourage teamwork; and (7) Have a habitual program of self-renewal. An additional established habit of Osler's was to be upbeat, to see life from the sunny side. That attitude was not only winsome, it was contagious, and meant he got along well with associates, students and residents.

The spoke of **Health**, brings to mind the statement of the Roman poet Juvenal: ***Mens sana in corpore sano*** (a sound

---

[2] The student life.

[3] Covey (1989).

mind in a sound body). It is axiomatic that those who would give advice to others about health matters should exemplify a sound mind in a sound body. One area of particular relevance to physicians concerns abuse of drugs and alcohol, both of which are especially accessible to doctors. Enslavement to either can be career-ending, and acting under the influence of either is a grave disservice to us and to our patients. (See also the section on TEMPERANCE.)

Family was a different consideration in Osler's time: medical students were not married and house officers basically lived in the hospital (consider the original meaning of resident!), as noted above. Nowadays the majority of medical students are married before they graduate, and many have begun raising a family. Parenting is a challenge for married medical students and residents. Many spouses work and providing family time together is a priority; not infrequently, both spouses work in the medical field. By the current generation, raising a family is a shared responsibility requiring flexibility in schedules. And as noted above (on page 80) by explorer Richard Byrd, a supportive family is a haven in the storms of life.

Finances have become a huge issue in the lives of medical students because of the cost of medical school tuition and accumulated debt at graduation. A recent survey[4] reported that 40% of first-year residents carried debt over $200K; for another 20% it was over $100K. Only 22% had *no* debt. The average salary for a male resident was $57K and for a woman, it was $56. Only eight percent reported that potential earnings would *not* influence their choice of a specialty.

Recognizing what it means to be a part of the **Profession** of medicine is an unfolding experience for every medical student

---

[4] Done by Medscape for May and June 2016, published online July 20, 2016.

and depends greatly on **mentoring** relationships established during those years. Those two topics are discussed in sections in this book at pages 13 and 149, respectively.

Recreation is important to self-renewal in a busy life. The long hours traditionally put in by students and residents have been somewhat ameliorated by adopting the "80-hour work-week," and fatigue is less of a problem than it once was. (Spending fewer hours at work affords students and residents more leisure, but it is arguable whether this makes for a superior educational experience. The debate is especially heated in surgical fields.) Patient safety may even be compromised due to problems with hand-offs on call, because fewer covering physicians have greater numbers of patients to care for, most of whom they do not know well at all.

Although less emphasis was placed on "physical fitness" in Osler's day than is presently the case, Osler had much to say about health maintenance and care of our body:

> **Learn early to take the best possible care of the machine, never over-driving it, nor letting rust or dust collect in the bearings, and providing it with enough fuel to keep it going at a fair pace. Unlike any ordinary mechanism, the more you use it, the more, within limits, you can get out of it. Healthy action in a body out of which you can get plenty of work is the great asset in the race, the most important part, perhaps, of life's reserves.**[5]

Osler encouraged prospective physicians to *have a hobby and ride it hard*. He wrote **"No man is really happy or safe**

---

[5] The reserves of life.

without a hobby, and it makes precious little difference what the outside interest may be—botany, beetles or butterflies, roses, tulips or irises; fishing, mountaineering or antiquities—anything will do so long as he straddles a hobby and rides it hard."[6] Osler's hobby was collecting books. He left his library to his alma mater at McGill (now called the *Bibliotheca Osleriana*). Organizing his books—7,000 of them including 104 incunabula (books published before the year 1501)—became a major source of solace during Osler's last years, after he had lost his son in the Great War. Osler also had a talent for collecting friends and kept in touch with many of them over his long life.

The **Social** life of physicians is one of its most satisfying aspects. The friendships one makes in medical school and

Grace, Revere, and William Osler in their backyard at 13 Norham Gardens, Oxford.

---

[6] The medical library in post-graduate work.

residency are long-lasting, and friendships made later in professional societies are often renewed annually at meetings. Osler was exemplary and extraordinary in his hospitality, which enhanced his effectiveness as a mentor. He and his wife Grace often entertained medical students and physicians in their homes, in Baltimore (at 1 West Franklin Street) and Oxford (at 13 Norham Gardens), but they cared little for "high society." By all accounts, Osler's marriage was agreeable, but few women today would subordinate their own interests to the extent that Grace Osler subordinated hers to a man so devoted to the many facets of a medical career. As was true of most marriages during that era, the husband was devoted to his career, and his wife was devoted to him.

Regarding **Spiritual** aspects in the balanced life, Osler asserted that **"Nothing in life is more wonderful than faith."**[7] We discuss spiritual matters more fully in the separate sections titled FAITH, HOPE, and LOVE. Osler did not wear his religion on his sleeve—see comment of Bliss (page 81).

One last thought regarding spiritual aspects of life relates to what we desire. What ought we to wish for as we set out to become physicians? There is a lesson in the life of Solomon as related in the Old Testament.[8] It seems to me, as I have observed successful practitioners, the answer is found in the story of Solomon's dream, as it's described in the Old Testament Book of First Kings. In that account, God expresses willingness to grant the new king whatever he desires, and He asks Solomon what he wishes for. Solomon asks not for long life or riches for himself, but for understanding to discern justice for his people. God is pleased with Solomon's answer and says,

---

[7] The faith that heals.
[8] First Kings 3:5-14.

"Because you have asked this thing...I have given you a wise and understanding heart... And I have also given you what you have not asked: both riches and honor..."

Similarly, in our experience, your desire is to put your patients first, given a reasonable level of skill and competence, you will have a prosperous, satisfying practice.

PATIENT AND PHYSICIAN

HUMANIZING THE PATIENT

T ry this thought experiment: Suppose you were found down on the sidewalk of a distant city, stabilized by paramedics, taken to a hospital, and admitted to a ward. What would you want caregivers to know about you as a person, not just a physiological preparation?

We feel strongly that, apart from emergency situations, the clinician should be interested in the *human* (not strictly medical) dimensions of the patient at hand. Indeed, CSB habitually taught medical students, "Your task is to make this patient seem like the most interesting human being in this county—a person that *everyone* should feel privileged to help!" This need not take a lot of time. When meeting a new patient in a non-urgent situation, even when you feel time-pressured, just ask a few questions, starting with "Where were you born?" Then, begin your history or consultation note with some interesting stuff that gives other caregivers a conversational ice-breaker. Here, for example, is an opening paragraph in a write-up for a patient:

> This 90-year-old man, who is a World War II veteran (navigator on a B-26 bomber in the European theater), an engineer by training, a retired administrator for a mental health system, who lives independently with his

wife of 65 years, and who has three children, eight grandchildren, and two great-great grandchildren, is seen in consultation with Dr. Blank for evaluation of acute septic arthritis of the left knee with positive cultures for *Staphylococcus aureus*.

Contrast that more personalized account with how such a patient is often introduced nowadays in a case presentation:

This is a 90-year-old-male with an infected knee.

Some (erroneously) consider the second example to be more objective. It is not. If your patient is a man, say <u>man</u>, (not male) or even better, give his occupation: we are dealing with humans. (If you have taken the additional, brief time to personalize your history, you will help humanize your patient for others. Moreover, if you try to see the problem as his own peculiar *illness* rather than just a specific *disease* that you are trying to diagnose, it will reap rich dividends in your relationship with him.)

Some trace today's fast-paced style of inpatient medicine to the 1983 Medicare legislation that introduced hospital reimbursement according to diagnosis-related groups (DRGs). Hospitals got paid a flat rate, so if a patient had a short stay the hospital made more money. In 1985 sociologist Terry Mizrahi coined the acronym GROP for "get rid of patients,"[1] reinforced by a peer culture in residency programs that encouraged objectification of patients and left no time as "the right time to acquire humanistic doctor-patient relationship skills." However, these problems are not new. In 1987 historian Charles Rosenberg entitled his book on the rise of hospitals in the U.S. *The Care of Strangers.*[2] He

---

[1] Mizrahi (1986).
[2] Rosenberg (1987).

recorded such observations by nineteenth-century physicians as "the patients fly by us like comets." (Does this sound familiar?) To reiterate, obtaining a meaningful social history need not take a lot of time and pays huge dividends down the road. The legendary California internist-teacher Faith Fitzgerald recounts this story of doing morning rounds at San Francisco General Hospital.[3]

Determined to teach the residents that "there are no uninteresting patients, just uninterest*ed* doctors," she asked a resident to choose the *least* interesting patient on the service. The patient turned out to be a monosyllabic elderly woman who'd been admitted to the hospital because she'd been evicted from her apartment and had nowhere else to go. Per the house officer's presentation, her life had been humdrum and she had no great stories. Dr. Fitzgerald asked (here in compressed quotes), "Have you ever been to a hospital before?" "Once," she answered. "What for?" "I broke my arm." "How did you break your arm?" "A trunk fell on it." "What kind of trunk?" "A steamer trunk." "How did that happen?" "The boat lurched." "Why did the boat lurch?" "It hit an iceberg." "What was the name of the boat?" "The *Titanic*." Suddenly the least-interesting patient on the teaching service instantly became the most interesting person in the San Francisco Bay Area! It was confirmed that as a girl from Ireland she'd been a steerage passenger on the *Titanic*! Finally, the residents took interest—as did the newspapers and television stations—in one of the last *Titanic* survivors!

Dr. Fitzgerald amply illustrated the sustained value of Rudyard Kipling's "six honest serving men": "I keep six honest serving men / (they taught me all I knew); /Their names are What and Why and When / and How and Where and Who." Parenthetically, the British physician Richard Asher has written a splendid essay[4] about how to incorporate that quatrain into one's history or case description.

---

[3] Fitzgerald (1999).

[4] Asher (1972) 54.

There is within medical education a growing movement to teach "reflective writing" to medical students. Pioneered by such educators as Jack Coulehan[5] and Rita Charon,[6] there is now wide appreciation that obtaining patients' illness narratives fosters "reflective practice" or "mindful practice," by which is meant the cultivation of self-awareness about what we do and why we do it. This practice has its own acronym, REFLECT.[7] In theory, at least, such exercises should enhance and enrich patient-physician relationships. Osler would no doubt encourage such exercises; he would also tell us that the concept is hardly new.

Like today's teachers, Osler warned: **"There is a tendency among young men about hospitals to study the cases, not the patients, and in the interest they take in the disease lose sight of the individual. Strive against this."**[8] Speaking informally to students at Oxford, he told them, **"in my behavior to my patients I make no difference whatever between the high and the low, between a duchess and a cook."**[9]

One of our major points, and a point well-illustrated by Dr. Fitzgerald's interview, concerns the strong desirability of *honoring* the patient. In the Hebrew Bible (Old Testament) is found the memorable line, "Honor the physician for the need thou hast of him" (Ecclesiasticus 38:1). We feel strongly that the patient should be similarly honored. This becomes especially important—and also clinically useful when dealing with patient's families in end-of-life situations. Take the time to sit down with family members and review the patient's life (asking them to bring in photographs, if another conference is to be scheduled)

---

[5] Coulehan and Granek (2012).
[6] Charon and Hermann (2012).
[7] Wald et al (2012).
[8] Gardner (1969).
[9] The student life.

and seek out interesting and affirming details of the patients' life story, the person they knew before he/she became just another patient with a grim prognosis.

To illustrate this point, CSB recently helped care for a man who was comatose from irreversible septic shock in the context of chronic liver disease secondary to alcoholism and hepatitis C. During a meeting with the patient's mother, son, and wife (from whom he'd been long separated), it was learned that he'd held a series of responsible jobs: meat cutter in a grocery store, lawn maintenance service operator, custodian of a church where he'd had a room on the property and house painter. Someone then volunteered that the patient had been a fixture in the public library, where he'd sit for hours reading *National Geographic* and other periodicals. "Everybody in the library knew him," they agreed. Obtaining this information and documenting it in the patient's record seemed to help everyone (health care providers included) become reconciled to a good death without heroic interventions. The patient died shortly thereafter.

For compassionate physicians, when we walk with a patient or a family through the Valley of the Shadow, a bit of us dies, too. After those times, it is wise to take time out to reflect and learn the lessons to be taught, perhaps sharing our sorrow with a friend or mentor. In a 2016 *JAMA* article[10] entitled "The things we have lost," the author reflected thoughtfully on such times.

Again, remember what most of us told (in one variation or another) a medical school's Admissions Committee: "I like science and I want to help people." Humanize the patient! It will make a difference in your career, and your professional life will be more enjoyable.

---

[10] Best JA (2016).

THE MEDICAL HISTORY

Osler sometimes receives credit for aphoristic sayings that are difficult to document. A common example is **"Listen to the patient, he is telling you the diagnosis."** Whether Osler actually said this is immaterial; it's still great advice. He stressed the centrality of the patient in medical education: **"In what may be called the natural method of teaching the student begins with the patient, continues with the patient, and ends his studies with the patient, using books and lectures as tools, as means to an end."**[1] He taught: **"Every patient you see is a lesson in much more than the malady from which he suffers."**[2] He gave practical advice: **"In taking histories follow each line of thought; ask no leading questions; never suggest. Give the patient's own words in the complaint."**[3] But apart from this emphasis on what is commonly called *attentive listening*, he left for us little specific advice about how he went about the process. Perhaps Osler emphasized the history because there were relatively few laboratory studies, and almost no imaging studies, to direct his focus elsewhere.

Most people would prefer their doctors to listen to them, and most medical educators stress this point, but patients often come

---

[1] The hospital as a college.

[2] The student life.

[3] Bean (1950).

away dissatisfied because we don't hear them out. Two separate studies indicated that while physicians often start out with open-ended questions, they interrupt patients on average just 12 seconds into the interview. What a shame! Occasional patients ramble incessantly, but, according to one study, most patients if uninterrupted will conclude their monologues within 30 seconds in primary care and within 90 seconds in consultant setting.[4] Think about it—how would *you* prefer to be treated? Permitting the patient an uninterrupted opening monologue, suppressing your impulse to ask targeted questions based on the diagnostic hypotheses forming in your mind—pays huge dividends. Your willingness to listen without interrupting tells your patients that you are receptive; conversely, cutting them off often leads them to NOT share important facts or happenings.

There is no single best method for taking a medical history. We suggest that readers (1) take seriously the recommendations of their own teachers and mentors; (2) self-monitor their skills at attentive listening; and (3) seek continual improvement in their ability to obtain and document their histories. In the meantime, here are our suggestions for taking the *history of the present illness*:

William Osler reviewing patients' records at the Johns Hopkins Hospital.

- Unless the situation is an emergency, sit down, make eye contact, act as though

---

[4] Rabinowitz et al (2004).

you have "all the time in the world" (even when you don't), and ask an open-ended question such as "Why are you here?"

- If you've had the luxury of reviewing the patient's record ahead of time, pause a moment before entering the room and consider how the patient might *feel* in light of what you now know. Then, begin your interview with a statement such as "I see you have _____; you must be feeling _____." Then, sit back and let the patient talk. (Often astute consultants purposely do *not* review the record in advance so they are unbiased.)

- Record the patient's chief complaint verbatim.

- Since your task is to obtain and record a *story*—a chronicle of the patient's illness—make your aim the *telling of the story* in a logical sequence. To this end, we find it helpful to begin by drawing a line down the center of a blank piece of paper. This will be your *timeline* for the patient's illness. As you obtain information from the patient (or from the medical record), indicate the time (with an arrow) to the left of the timeline, and then record the patient's account (or information gleaned from the medical record) to the right of the timeline.

- Record key statements from patients in *their own word*s. Don't assign medical terms to the patient's words (unless, of course, the patient uses medical terms).

- Ask the patient, "When was the last time you were in your usual state of good health?" You may need to ask this question again and again, like a lawyer drilling a witness, to ascertain when the illness actually began. Problems that initially seem to be acute may actually be subacute or chronic, or they might have a prodrome that will prove essential to determining the diagnosis.

- After you're satisfied that you've taken a complete history of the present illness, consider asking the patient "What do *you* think is wrong?"
- Two additional questions are often worthwhile. Asking "How has this illness affected you?" will help bring out its meaning to your patient. Asking a related question, "What is your <u>greatest fear</u> concerning this illness?" will help you assess its emotional impact and also may give you the chance later to offer reassurance. Many patients have unwarranted fears that cause unnecessary anxiety.
- If the patient has had similar illnesses in the past, explore how these resembled the present illness and also how they differed.

Next, take the *past medical history*, beginning with "How has your health been *most* of your life, except for this illness?" Record the response verbatim. A stoic might answer "Excellent!" A person with somatization disorder might answer, "Mama said I was sickly even as a baby." Document all hospitalizations and operations. If the patient gives a history of drug allergy, ask exactly what happened and how long ago it occurred. Then, obtain a *review of systems* and make note of what might be relevant to the present illness. Don't forget the family history and the social history. These, too, can be relevant to diagnosing the present illness and can also help with one of your essential functions: counseling.

Here are a few style pointers for writing up the history of the present illness:

- After stating the patient's name at the beginning of your write-up, refer to the patient as *he* or *she*. Don't say "the patient" over and over. *Who else but the patient?*

- Write a lead paragraph that frames the scenario, answers most if not all of Kipling's "six honest serving men" (see page 99), and incorporates the chief complaint verbatim along with the duration of the illness. Include such things as the patient's age, marital status, and occupation. Include previous diagnoses that might be relevant (e.g., "whose previous diagnoses include") but make a note that your task is to verify each of these diagnoses, since they could be wrong! For example:

- Using the timeline that you developed to obtain the patient's story, write (or dictate) the HPI as series of short paragraphs. Emulate Ernest Hemingway, not William Faulkner. The long, unbroken paragraph seems to be the norm nowadays. In our opinion, segmenting the HPI into a series of short paragraphs arranged in logical sequence according to the date of occurrence makes for a more readable HPI.

- Begin each of the first several paragraphs with a participial phrase denoting time. Thus, the first paragraph might begin: "Three weeks ago, he was in his usual state of fair health when he noted the onset of increasing shortness of breath, and also swelling of his feet as the day progressed." The second paragraph might similarly begin: "Twelve days ago, he consulted his primary care physician and was told his heart failure seemed to be somewhat worse. A chest X-Ray was obtained and his dose of diuretic was increased."

- Finally, incorporate relevant aspects of the review of systems.

Develop your own style. Just as each patient is unique, so every physician brings his or her particular experience to the interview. Strive to make your write-up a pleasure for the next person to read, and a valuable tool for care of your patient!

THE PHYSICAL EXAM[1]

O sler was trained in the naturalist tradition; that is, the basic method was to observe carefully, then reason from the observations. Observation, however, is an acquired skill. **"The whole art of medicine is in observation ... but to educate the eye to see, the ear to hear and the finger to feel takes time, and to make a beginning, to start [students] on the right path is all that we can do" ... "give them good methods and a proper point of view, and all other things will be added as [their] experience grows."[2]**

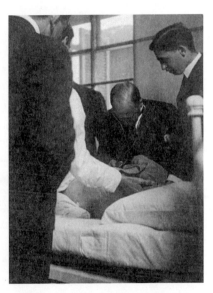

William Osler listening to a patient's heart at the bedside at the Johns Hopkins Hospital.

---

[1] This chapter is written by JBV.

[2] On the need of a radical reform in our methods of teaching senior students.

For purposes of discussion, let us consider the physical exam (PE) in two parts: A) The Annual Physical Exam; and B) The Physical Exam as a diagnostic modality.

A) The annual physical exam has come in for some hard knocks lately.[3] It's considered by some bloggers as too time-consuming and a waste of money. But the annual visit to one's doctor—to include a brief, focused—physical exam—still serves a useful purpose, just as an annual visit to one's dentist does. It brings the doctor up to date regarding the patient's health and allows addressing any questions the patients may have about medications or any new symptoms. I visit my primary physician about every 18 months and welcome his input regarding any specialist consultants I may need. I find it money well spent.

B) Regarding the PE itself, I have found it valuable for a number of reasons, as noted below. I was "weaned" on an early edition of Hamilton Bailey's superb monograph *Physical Signs in Clinical Surgery*,[4] and I found that developing the skills of careful examination and observation during medical school and residency improved my diagnostic acumen and made me a better surgeon. Some thoughts:

- *A well-done PE promotes confidence and compliance.* During seven years teaching emergency medicine, I showed students and residents how to do a "90 Second PE" to evaluate trauma victims. I found when applied

---

[3]   http://montrealgazette.com/news/local-news/quebec-to-do-away-with-annual-health-checkups
[4]   Available today as the 19th edition, *Hamilton Bailey's Demonstrations of Physical Signs in Clinical Surgery*. Boca Raton, FL: CRC Press © 2016.

to other, non-trauma patients in the ED, they seemed more trusting and more apt to follow my instructions. Conversely, after consulting a urologist for a particular problem of my own, my confidence in him waned when he omitted a physical exam, simply telling me my PSA was O.K. I expected a more thorough evaluation and thought less of him for his omission.

- *A PE can be more reliable than an X-Ray.* Two examples stand out in my memory, and both brought to mind a sign printed in calligraphy in my medical school's radiology department: *"We see what we look for, we recognize what we know."* First was an Indian woman I saw in my office when I served in the Indian Health Service (IHS). She was told to come for removal of stitches in her knee following an auto accident 10 days earlier. Her husband brought her in to the exam room in a wheelchair and helped her up on the table. She was in pain and had a red bandanna tied to her ankle with which he lifted her leg as she lay back supine. It was immediately evident, when I asked her to lift her leg, that she had a mid-shaft fracture of the femur. It had been missed on the night of the accident by the orthopedist called to care for her. He had done an X-Ray but misread it, overlooking a sharp spicule of bone hidden by the top of the view box. The radiologist who read the film the next morning in our small hospital also missed it. But the break would have been evident on PE. (I suspect alcohol was involved that may have blunted her pain.) She had been a front seat passenger without a seat belt and the laceration from impacting the dashboard was classic. It is often associated with femoral fracture or hip dislocation, both of which are evident on PE—if you look for them!

- A second situation was that of my own seven-year-old daughter when she was injured in a head-on collision. I was on my way back to Portland from San Francisco as my wife was driving to the airport. I went at once to the small hospital where the family had been taken and found two of my surgical colleagues there, summoned by the moonlighting resident. In evaluating my daughter—who had been restrained by a lap-belt in the back seat—found a tender bruise along her lumbar spine, which in association with her tender abdomen, meant she had suffered an acute flexion injury in which the small bowel was torn, compressed against the sacral promontory. Simultaneously, the flexion ruptured the posterior longitudinal ligament of the spine. A plain, A-P X-Ray of her abdomen was read as normal, when in actuality she had a severe compression fracture of L-3. The radiologist did not count the vertebrae (it appeared normal, but there were only four instead of five, due to the compression), so he missed the diagnosis—which was evident on PE.

- *An astute PE may reveal unsuspected malignancy.* Consider the finding of a "Sister Mary Joseph nodule."[5] The eponym came from a nun, a nurse who was prepping a patient's abdomen for a diagnostic laparotomy in the operating room of surgeon W. J. Mayo. She noticed a subcutaneous nodule near the umbilicus. It turned out to be a tumor nodule metastatic from a carcinoma of the pancreas. It was 1928, long before CTs or MRIs; but even today, finding such a nodule on your physical exam would be highly significant, indicating a stage IV intra-abdominal malignancy (gastric, pancreatic, ovarian, or colonic).

---

[5] http://www.nejm.org/doi/full/10.1056/NEJMicm040708#t=article

- ***Well-applied PE skills may save a life.*** Late one evening when I was on duty as a resident in the ED, a young man was brought in who'd been stabbed in the chest near the sternum in a barroom fight. It happened that I had recently read an article about stab wounds of the heart, and I recognized the symptoms and signs of pericardial tamponade—increasing apprehension, dilated neck veins with normal breath sounds on both sides, with a narrowing pulse pressure—just like my patient. I'd never done a pericardiocentesis before, but the article I'd read had illustrative diagrams and the experienced nurse had gotten the setup ready. The patient was rapidly deteriorating so I went ahead. I drew off 60 ml of blood, and he improved, just as the thoracic surgery resident (whom we had stat paged) arrived. He took the patient to the OR and sewed up a small laceration of the right ventricle.

- Paying attention to the PE enhances our observational skills. In my surgical practice I saw a 35-year-old woman referred for a thrombosed external hemorrhoid.[6] Ostensibly, she needed evacuation of the clot, but on my PE I noticed she was wearing an engagement ring with a 6-point Tiffany setting (like my wife's). But in hers, the stone was gone. As I inquired about that, she began to cry and related she had just separated from her husband. Her marital problems were a greater problem than her hemorrhoid, and after removing the clot under local anesthetic we referred her to a counselor.

- A careful PE can be the key to the diagnosis. The importance of keen observation is worth emphasizing.

---

[6] http://emedicine.medscape.com/article/775407-clinical

In his charming little book,[7] British Surgeon Sir Zachary Cope (1881-1974) commented "More things are missed because you do not look than from not knowing what is in the book."

JAMA[8] published a recent example. Dr. Robert Hirschtick describes the case of an elderly woman who had chest pain presented to him by the house staff. The diagnosis was obscure despite normal troponin levels and serial ECGs. He began his bedside exam by slightly lowering her hospital gown to auscultate her heart (unlike the resident, the intern and the student, all of whom, it turned out, had listened through her clothing in a "quick physical exam"). Immediately the dermatomal vesicular rash of herpes zoster was apparent, which established the diagnosis.

Likewise, Osler said:

> **Science has been defined as the habit or faculty of observation . . . Only a quantitative difference— accuracy—makes observation scientific.** (He went on to elaborate) **The Hunterian *"Do not think, but try"*[9] attitude of mind is the important one to cultivate. The question came up one day when discussing the grooves left on the nails after a fever, how long it took for the nail to grow out, from root to edge. A majority of the class had no further interest; a few looked it up**

---

[7] Cope Z (1947). Cope wrote the book to accompany his classic volume *The Early Diagnosis of the Acute Abdomen*, (1921) available as a 2005 edition from Amazon, edited by Silen.

[8] Hirschtick RE (2016).

[9] When Surgeon John Hunter (1728-93) was told by his former pupil Edward Jenner (1749-1823) that he thought having cowpox made milkmaids immune to smallpox, Hunter offered that famous piece of advice.

**in books; two men marked their nails at the root with
nitrate of silver, and a few months later had positive
knowledge on the subject. They showed the proper
spirit.**[10]

So become the best physical diagnostician you can! It will
have surprising rewards and make you a better physician.

---

[10] The student life.

DIAGNOSIS[1]

The physician must answer three questions: What is wrong with the patient? (Diagnosis) What can I do for the patient? (Therapeutic Plan) What will be the outcome in this unique individual patient? (Prognosis) Osler touched on all three of these during an 1885 address to medical students:

> **Two thoughts should ever be in your minds: how can I best recognize and how can I best treat disease.... [Another] element must always be taken into account in prognosis and that is the personal equation of the patient. No two cases of the same disease are ever alike; the constitution of the person, his individuality, stamps each case with certain peculiarities.[2]**

Diagnosis comes first. A secure diagnosis makes therapeutic options straightforward; we can look them up in readily-available sources such as textbooks (or Up-to-Date ®). Osler stressed the primacy of diagnosis: **"In the fight which we have to wage incessantly against ignorance and quackery among the**

---

[1] This chapter is by CSB.

[2] Unpublished draft of an address to medical students at the University of Pennsylvania, 1885.

masses and follies of all sorts among the classes, *diagnosis*, not *drugging*, is our chief weapon of offense."[3]

An incredible array of blood tests and imaging procedures makes diagnosis much easier than it was during Osler's day. Consider Osler's *Lectures on the Diagnosis of Abdominal Tumors*, which were given in 1893. We marvel at his detailed histories and physical examinations yet we conclude that most of his diagnoses would be easily made nowadays by some combination of CT scans, endoscopic procedures, and/or percutaneous biopsies. Consider also a volume published 80 years later, in 1973, by the renowned Johns Hopkins internist Philip A. Tumulty, entitled *The Effective Clinician: His Methods and Approach to Diagnosis and Care*,[4] in which Tumulty discusses his approach to 20 tough cases using the format of the clinico-pathological conference (CPC). Reviewing the cases today,[5] we note that two of them did not really present diagnostic dilemmas and that in a third case the diagnosis would now be different. Of the remaining 17 cases today's technology would quickly resolve at least 13 before or shortly after admission

William Osler contemplating at a patient's bedside at the Johns Hopkins Hospital.

---

[3] Chauvinism in medicine.

[4] Tumulty (1973).

[5] Bryan (2000).

to the hospital. The generalist-physician's role as master diagnostician has shrunk considerably since Osler's day—or has it?

At least three considerations reinforce the continued need for thoughtful approach to diagnosis. First, one must consider the context of the disease: the individual patient. Osler stressed this point, as evinced by comments in two addresses given nine years apart: **"As no two faces, so no two cases are alike in all respects and unfortunately it is not only the disease itself which is so varied, but the subjects themselves have peculiarities which modify its action"**[6]; and **"Variability is the law of life, and as no two faces are the same, so no two bodies are alike, and no two individuals react alike and behave alike under the abnormal conditions which we know as disease."**[7] Moreover:

> **As clinical observers, we study the experiments which Nature makes upon our fellow-creatures. These experiments, however, in striking contrast to those of the laboratory, lack exactness, possessing as they do a variability at once a despair and a delight—the despair of those who look for nothing but fixed laws in an art which is still deep in the sloughs of Empiricism; the delight of those who find in it an expression of a universal law transcending, even scorning, the petty accuracy of test-tube and balance, the law that in man "the measure of all things," mutability, variability, mobility, are the very marrow of his being.**[8]

The variability of disease in different patients makes

---

[6] Teaching and thinking.

[7] On the educational value of the medical society.

[8] Teaching and thinking.

some investigators question the extent to which results of prospective, randomized, controlled trials apply to real-life clinical practice, especially in older adults who over time accumulate numerous medical problems (that is, confounding variables to the conclusions of even the best-designed studies).

A second consideration involves the extent to which newer diagnostic modalities may actually *increase* the potential for error. We highly recommend a paper by Donald A. Redelmeier entitled "The cognitive psychology of missed diagnoses"[9] or a book by Jerome Groopman entitled *How Doctors Think*,[10] both of which shed insight into how we process information, reason, and draw conclusions that may or may not be correct. As it turns out, all of us develop shortcuts in reasoning ("heuristics") that generally serve us quite well but also predispose us to serious errors. Even experienced clinicians must guard against the possibility that their initial diagnoses might be erroneous. (See Table on page 118.) All of us are predisposed to "framing effects" and "blind obedience to human authority," especially when these come in the form of written reports by other physicians, especially reports by radiologists and pathologists. Too often we turn to these colleagues as though they were the Oracle of Delphi. We forget that they, like us, must often make judgment calls based on incomplete data. Groopman after reviewing the literature asserts that currently "the average diagnostic error in interpreting medical images is in the twenty percent to thirty percent range" and that such errors (whether false-negative or false-positive) "have significant impact on patient care." Likewise, he cites a study in which 13 pathologists read 1,001 biopsies of the cervix, and later went back over the same specimens: "On average, each

---

[9] Redelmeier (2005).

[10] Groopman (2007).

Table. COMMON CAUSES OF MISSED DIAGNOSES*		
Type of Error	Definition	Clinical maxim
Premature closure	Adhesion to a single idea	Think: "What's the one diagnosis I don't want to miss here?"
Anchoring heuristic**	Reliance on initial impression	Ask: "If this person were to die unexpectedly, what would the autopsy show?"
Framing effects	Being unduly influenced by subtle wording†	"Is there another angle?" "Let's play devil's advocate here."
Blind obedience to human authority	Unwarranted deference to authority	"Should I bring this up tactfully with the source?" "Should I get another opinion?"
Blind obedience to technology	Unwarranted reliance on technology†	"What is the diagnostic accuracy of this technology?"
Availability heuristic**	Judgment based on previous experience	"Does my experience accurately reflect this patient's condition?" "If you hear hoof beats in a barnyard, think of horses, not zebras."

*Modified after Redelmeier (2005).
**"Heuristic" is used here as "a short-cut in reasoning that allows one to solve problems rapidly."
†Wording in radiology, pathology, and laboratory reports can lead to serious errors.

pathologist agreed with himself only 89 percent of the time, and with a panel of senior pathologists only 87 percent of the time." It should be clear from such data that we must constantly be on guard to avoid errors. Form a habit of reviewing X-Rays, CTs and MRIs with a radiologist; don't just read the report. Osler knew this well:

> **Various degrees of probability we may attain to and do reach daily but in the busy round of teaching and practice we are apt to forget that positive certainty until we have a rude awakening and a useful lesson in the folly of over-confidence. . . . Come to the study of the diagnosis of disease with all the modesty at your command. Positiveness and dogmatism are inevitable associates of superficial knowledge in medicine.**[11]

And mark this well: **"Absolute diagnoses are unsafe, and are made at the expense of the conscience."**[12] Along this line Osler made a suggestion that remains highly useful:

> **Begin early to make a threefold category—clear cases, doubtful cases, mistakes. And learn to play the game fair, no self-deception, no shrinking from the truth; mercy and consideration for the other man, but for yourself, you have to keep an incessant watch. You remember Lincoln's famous *mot* about the impossibility of fooling all of the people all of the time. It does not hold good for the individual who can fool himself to his heart's content all of the time.**[13]

---

[11] Unpublished draft of an address to medical students at the University of Pennsylvania.

[12] Bean (1950), 129.

[13] The student life.

Here are a few suggestions:

- Once you've done a complete history and a careful physical exam, make a habit of formulating further studies (Lab, X-Rays, scans, etc.) by considering first those that are the simplest, least invasive and least expensive. A recent case discussed in JAMA[14] concerned a man with recurrent pneumonia who was losing weight, but on whom many expensive scans had turned up nothing. As a last resort a hospital pulmonologist ordered an inexpensive sputum cytology. It gave the diagnosis of lung cancer and could have been done much earlier.
- In reviewing a medical record, note the previous diagnoses but also review *how* each diagnosis was reached. Once a diagnosis has been made, it tends to be perpetuated by observer after observer. This is especially likely to happen with the electronic medical record (EMR). Ask questions. Challenge each diagnosis. Satisfy yourself that the patient's problem list is accurate.
- When making a diagnosis, use modifiers. Today's coding and billing procedures force us to use definite terms in situations that are often unclear. Our suggestion is to use modifiers. For example: "Pneumonia, suspected, with pulmonary infiltrate and low-grade fever, improvement while on antibiotics, see discussion below" (noting in the discussion, perhaps, that blood cultures were sterile, that non-infectious causes of pulmonary infiltrates had not been rigorously excluded, and that certain "send-out"

---

[14] Bebell LM (2016).

specimens were pending).

- Review and record your experience, as Osler did, noting "clear cases," "doubtful cases," and "mistakes." Keep a journal: make notes and regularly review them.

Finally, make a practice of making an initial diagnosis, and then comparing it against your final diagnosis after everything has been said and done. With time, your confidence will grow and you'll find yourself relying more on clinical judgment and less on expensive tests and procedures and the opinions of consultants!

THE ART OF PRESENTATION[1]

O ne of the most important aspects of being a physician is to actively listen to our patients' stories and to be a good storyteller ourselves. Presenting a patient is a unique style of storytelling, a critical tool for collaboration. Frankly, it is how your colleagues—student, resident, or attending—are going to judge you.

Know Your Audience

Before you present a patient you want to collect your thoughts and be clear that you've got the information you need. You should also know your audience. If in the ambulatory setting, is this a sick or well visit? If an inpatient in the hospital, is this the admission history and physical or a subsequent hospital stay visit? You want to be specialty specific. How you present to an OB GYN attending will warrant different information than to a cardiologist. Likewise, a formal presentation on medical service rounds will be more robust, than describing someone with sinusitis in the ambulatory setting. However, the same format should be followed. The "SOAP" (Subjective, Objective, Assessment, and Plan) note is ideal and a standard in how physicians communicate.

---

[1] This chapter is by Richard Colgan, M.D.

Begin by noting the primary reason why the patient sought attention, their chief complaint. It's often best to put this in the patient's own words.

The opening sentence of the history of present illness should be the most important. Don't hide the most important piece of information deep into your presentation. As journalists might say, don't "bury your lead." An example worth following might be: "This is the first hospital admission for this 23-year-old female, on oral contraceptive therapy, who developed acute onset of dry cough and shortness of breath after flying home from Colorado where she suffered a tibial plateau fracture after a fall skiing 3 days ago." Most seasoned clinicians would hear this sentence and say: "Hmm. She likely has a pulmonary embolus." The history of present illness is the "scaffold" on which your entire story is built. Include a chronology of when the problem started, how it has progressed and what is its current status. The listener should clearly be able to discern when the patient was well last. Tell us. In the words of William J. Mayo: "Begin with an arresting sentence, close with a strong summary; in between, speak simply, clearly, and always to the point, and above all be brief."

Don't Forget Your P's and Q's

Consider the following mnemonic when describing pain:
  P – provocative/palliative/prior treatment
  Q – quality
  R – region/radiation
  S – severity/other symptoms
  T – time: onset, duration, periodicity

Throughout the history of present illness you need to appreciate the power of the spoken word. Sell your story. You must believe what you are saying is important to the overall care of the patient. Bring in any pertinent positives and negatives. A pertinent positive in the above case would be to mention that the patient suffered worsening calf pain upon getting off of the airplane, or that she had a family history of first degree relatives who'd had thrombotic disorders at young ages.

In biology we are taught that form follows function. Another benefit of a succinct presentation which follows the SOAP format is that it forces you to not forget things. William Osler spoke to this in his essay "Teacher and Student."[2] In between urging that students practice the art of detachment and have the grace of humility, Osler advocated for the virtue of method and the quality of thoroughness. By striving to always present your patients in the same SOAP fashion you are being methodical. You are likely to not forget to ask about their allergies, for example. By describing the patient's physical exam from head to toe you are being thorough.

The Absolutes

Every presentation—whether calling from an emergency room to a consultant on call (a short presentation) or addressing an audience at medical grand rounds—should include at a minimum the following information:

Subjective: Chief complaint, history of present illness, medications, and allergies;

Objective: General appearance, vital signs, and pertinent positive and negative findings;

Assessment: What you think is going on;

Plan: What you want to do about it.

---

[2] Teacher and student.

Common mistakes that all clinicians make
(You will make them too!)

Some essential points must be made here—critical points. Younger clinicians often do not appreciate the following cautions, so let's disclose some secrets now.

First, don't overlook the general appearance—the "look of the patient." A woman who's reading a book as you walk into the room and does not look up as you enter is likely not as sick as another woman lying on her side, in the fetal position, eyes closed with tears running down her face. Your unschooled grandmother might suspect someone had a surgical abdomen—just based on the patient's appearance. It is a mistake to discount the general appearance. One of the most important admonitions of Hippocrates was to observe *all.* Osler, too, urged us to inspect, to palpate, to percuss, and to *contemplate.*

Second, those vital signs, well . . . THEY ARE VITAL! That's why they are called *vital signs!* Don't dismiss them, ignore them, or fail to mention them. Carefully taking the vital signs is often your first clue as to how sick your patient is. If they are normal? Fine, let the listener know if the vital signs are stable—if that is indeed true. And get in the habit of *personally* taking your patient's vital signs yourself.

Third, don't regurgitate your history and physical and call it an assessment. The point is: assume that whomever you present your history and physical to is listening. Don't just repeat your findings. The assessment is where you synthesize something that was not there before: you are creating something new. It's your working diagnosis of what you think is going on. What if you don't know what is going on? (Good question!) If that's true, say so. You are not obligated to know everything. If you are not sure why she is short of breath, say: dyspnea etiology unclear, followed by some possibilities from most likely to least likely.

Another example might be: Chest pain, cause unknown. You might offer up that this could be musculoskeletal or gastrointestinal in origin. However, given that a patient had all the known risk factors for cardiovascular disease and that this crushing mid sternal chest pain has been persistent since the patient finished his first marathon, to note that you are concerned for acute coronary syndrome is a good bet. Say so in your assessment. (Always remember Occam's razor, which states that medicine has a bias towards simple explanations. Common things really do occur more commonly. Consider that when formulating your assessment. In the words of the late, University of Maryland School of Medicine educator, Dr. Theodore Woodward: "If you hear hoof beats, don't turn around expecting to see a zebra. Expect a horse.")

Fourth, your plan can include diagnostics, therapeutics, educational, and preventive measures as well as when the patient should follow up. This is where you say what you are going to do, your recommended plan.

Finally, a common mistake is to not present in the proper order of S-O-A-P. Always go from S to O to A to P. Don't skip around or go back and forth. Once you've left the land of "S," like Toyland, you can never go back again. If you realize you've forgotten something, it's ok to say, "I forgot something. May I mention something else from the history?"

Following the above recommendations takes practice. The good news is that it's like riding a bike. You likely fell the first few times you attempted it, but with practice you became great at it. And rest assured, those to whom you present will think: Wow, s/he sounds like a doctor who knows what they are talking about. That's the key to any good story: along with saying it in the right order, you show you know what you are saying.

"MORE THAN JUST SKILL AND KNOWLEDGE"

Over time, it has been observed, the "hard subjects" of medical school (for example, the origins, insertions, and innervations of each muscle; the Krebs cycle; and the MHC molecules on antigen-presenting cells) become "soft," whereas the "soft subjects" (such as the patient-physician relationship, resolving ethical dilemmas, and communicating with family members) become "hard." This point was driven home to JBV in a story told about a lecture given by Dr. Francis C. Wood, who during the late 20th Century served 18 years as professor of medicine at the University of Pennsylvania (where Osler had taught a century earlier).

The story was told by Dr. Wood's son, who was also a physician. The older Dr. Wood, his son recalled, gave an annual lecture to fourth-year medical students. "To speak to a group of medical students on the subject of what a doctor needs besides medical skill and knowledge is first to admit that a doctor certainly needs that skill and knowledge. You will have to do a great deal of concentrated study to learn enough to be a doctor. You can't just be kind-hearted and stupid—you'll kill too many people." So did Dr. Wood open his lecture.

But *what else* do you need besides skill and knowledge? Here's what Dr. Wood said, according to his son Larry:

"In order to get a variety of ideas for my talk, I asked several of my patients to write their answers to this question. Strangely enough, they all said the same thing. Here is a [letter] which expresses it best. It was written by one of the most attractive intelligent women I have ever known [Dr. Wood withheld her name]." She wrote:

> When a person is sick, he is afraid—afraid of all the things a sickness may bring to him: pain, invalidism, heavy expenses, unpleasant and strange hospital experiences, hardship to his family, maybe death.
>
> Since fear and anxiety are not only extremely unpleasant sensations within themselves, but may also affect the patient's condition, the doctor's first need, after a sound knowledge of medicine, is to be able to alleviate the fear in his patient and substitute confidence. To do this adequately, he must be more than a skillful medical scientist. He must be an adult (man or woman) who has lived a sufficiently normal, well-rounded life to provide him with normal experiences. Out of these experiences and through reading comes understanding, and out of understanding comes confidence. Out of both comes the trained instinct that makes a doctor and helps him know how to talk to the particular individual before him.

Dr. Wood (senior) continued, "What I have concluded, tentatively, with all this thinking? Life and death are still mysteries to me. I do not have a blueprint of why things happen or how they happen. I agree with Dr. Grant Conklin who said, 'There is as much chance that life developed by accident as that Webster's Unabridged Dictionary resulted from an explosion in a printing plant.'

"What do I really admire and think important? Kindliness, friendliness, love, courage, tolerance, consideration, understanding, humility, and a twinkle in the eye—everything which seems to be important is non-material."[1]

---

[1] Wood (2004).

TOWARD THE END OF LIFE

None of us—patients and doctors—will live forever. We all die sometime, and how we deal with death relates not only to our own, personal experience, but also as doctors, to our concept of healing and what we see as our mission as physicians. If we see our job as only conquering disease and staving off death, we are ultimately to be defeated, for death claims all of us. No one escapes.

But if we take as a goal the maxim of Edward Livingston Trudeau (a respected physician who battled tuberculosis in the early twentieth century), we have a different outlook. Trudeau's goal was: ***To cure sometimes; to relieve often; to comfort always.*** Considering his words brings to mind the coda of St. Paul's "Hymn to Love" in First Corinthians, Chapter 13: ***And now abide faith, hope, love, these three; but the greatest of these is love.*** Patients come to us and have *faith* in us; and they *hope* for the best—to be relieved of their suffering and disease. When hope for cure is gone, we must comfort and *love* them to the end.

Too often we have seen situations where a doctor feels he has nothing more to offer, so in effect abandons the patient. Or a patient gets another round of toxic chemotherapy, curing nothing, causing more suffering, when we should be switching to palliative care. Dr. Howard Spiro observed that we doctors live at once in two conflicting worlds—"the world of science, which provides them with their knowledge of disease, very real advances against those diseases . . . and the world of people, with instincts, pain, suffering, hope and joy."[1]

Hear also what the contemporary surgeon-writer Atul Gawande writes in his best-selling 2014 book *Being Mortal*: "You don't have to spend much time with the elderly or those with terminal illness to see how often medicine fails the people it is supposed to help. The waning days of our lives are given over to treatments that addle our brains and sap our bodies for a sliver's chance of benefit." Gawande describes how he was taught in medical school how to save lives but not how to attend those whose lives were coming to an end. *Being Mortal* is a book[2] that every medical student and resident should read as preparation for learning about end-of-life care.

When hope for cure is gone, we can still bring comfort to our patients. As a surgeon (JBV), patients most often came to me because of some derangement in their *body*, caused by accident or illness. But I found illness was never restricted to bodily disease or trauma; it affected the whole person. And the key to promoting health and healing likewise was to deal with the whole person. I believe we are most whole and healthy when we are sound in body, mind and spirit, and are in right relationship to one another and with our Creator. I realized too that helping patients heal involved more than just repairing the body. Early in my career I learned an important lesson.

Called in consultation to see a woman I'll call Mrs. O., with advanced stage ovarian cancer, I was asked to insert a Hickman catheter to give central vein access for chemotherapy and pain

[1] Spiro (1998).
[2] Gawande (2014).

relief. The procedure went well, but her prognosis was of course guarded. On my rounds a week later, as I sat at the bedside to remove a stitch that had secured the catheter, I asked her a question that I sometimes ask patients whose prognosis is uncertain: "What would you like to see happen in the time you have left?" After a brief pause, she responded.

Her eyes welled up and out poured a heartrending story of alienation from her daughter, with whom she had not spoken for several months, since they'd had a falling out regarding one of the grandchildren. I was struck by the poignancy of her story and recalled seeing as I'd come on the ward one of the nurses dictating an off-shift report into a cassette recorder. A sudden thought occurred to me, and I said to Mrs. O.: "I would like to borrow the nurse's tape recorder and have you again relate the story you just told me. Then let us send it to your daughter." She was agreeable. We borrowed a spare cassette and I mailed it off that afternoon. A few days later as I entered her room on rounds, her face lit up.

"Oh Doctor! I have wonderful news. My daughter is coming to see me!" They indeed did have a healing in their relationship, and Mrs. O. was much more at peace when she faced death a few weeks later.

How do we know when to switch from attempting to cure to comfort care? It is not an easy decision. Plutarch tells an instructive story about the Roman general Marius who suffered from an affliction of boils on his legs, who called a surgeon to lance them. The doctor began on one leg, lancing several, working upward. As he was about to begin on the other leg, Marius held up his hand. "The cure is worse than the disease," he said, and stopped the surgeon from proceeding. The best way to know how our patients are doing is to keep asking questions, and listening carefully to their answers.

BREAKING BAD NEWS

On rare occasions we must convey a diagnosis with a poor prognosis, such as a situation of terminal cancer, or perhaps break the news to the family of a patient who has died in surgery. Here are some tips we have found helpful:

- Take time.
- Sit down. Have everyone sit down. Be prepared to listen as well as talk.
- Take a nurse or chaplain[3] with you, especially in death situations.
- Plan in advance what you will say. Consider all you know about the patient—personality, stamina, aspirations, as well as the diagnosis and the prognosis.
- Be gentle and loving; not abrupt, blunt, harsh, or cruel.
- Lead in slowly and recap the situation up to and including surgery; it's a good way to open the discussion.
- Tell the truth but emphasize the positive.
- (We cannot delegate giving bad news. It's our job.)

ASSISTED SUICIDE—AN OPTION?

As Co-Chair of a large medical center's bioethics committee at a time before palliative care became a specialty, and when hospice care was just getting started, JBV attended a conference in London in which Dr. Cecily Saunders (who founded the Hospice Movement in the U.K.) and Dr. Pieter Admiraal (who designed the euthanasia system in the Netherlands) were panelists. I knew quite a bit about hospice then, but nothing about euthanasia in

---

[3] VanderVeer (2012).

Holland, so I asked Dr. Admiraal if I could visit him and look at their system of euthanasia (E) and Physician-assisted suicide (PAS).

I made two trips to the Netherlands and published a review paper about their system.[4] I concluded that the two societies (U.S. and the Netherlands) were too different for E to take place here, but PAS might work with proper controls. Indeed, about the same time, Oregon enacted its Death with Dignity Act. Having practiced in Oregon, and having carried many of my patients through terminal diseases, I believe PAS has a limited application, and is worth reading about for students and residents. As we have seen palliative care improve and referrals to hospice occur earlier and more appropriately, the need for PAS should remain quite rare. In 2011 the AMA published a good review of end-of-life care.[5] In July 2016 JAMA published a clinical review of this subject.[6]

---

[4] VanderVeer (1999).
[5] JAMA (Eds.) (2011).
[6] Emanuel (2016).

THE TRAINING YEARS

CHOOSING FURTHER TRAINING

Today as they plan the course of their training, medical students must, relatively early, make a decision about specializing. It usually first involves deciding to pursue a medical or a surgical career. That choice puts you into a medical or surgical residency track. That choice, like others that follow, is aided by following the famous counsel of the Oracle at Delphi, namely, *Know thyself.*

Here for example, is how JBV went about deciding. I had broad interests—enjoying most of my sub-specialty rotations in medical school—and I liked people. I also liked working with my hands and I'd been a carpenter's apprentice during college summers. I liked to "wrap things up" rather than draw them out, so surgery appealed to me more than medicine. But frankly, I had a hard time deciding. So I took a university hospital rotating internship (a few of them existed in 1965), and because the Vietnam War was on (I didn't approve of it, plus had a wife and small daughter), I chose to serve in the Indian Health Service branch of the U.S. Public Health Service (USPHS). That gave me more time to decide (plus two extra years of general medical and pediatric experience); during that period I decided on surgery. Cardiac surgery and colorectal surgery appealed to me as I experienced them on resident rotations. I also did some ED moonlighting during my general surgical residency and enjoyed that exposure. When in my senior year my chief asked me to join the faculty and take charge of ED and trauma service at the University medical center (in Portland, Oregon), I did just that. The specialty of Emergency Medicine was just getting started and it was a great spot to teach students and residents, so I stayed on and made that my chosen field. I did, however, get my boards in surgery, so seven years later, when I chose to take up private practice in surgery, I made a smooth transition.

And here's how CSB decided. I fell in love with pathology during my sophomore year of medical school, and was among the students chosen to do their "free quarter" (10 weeks at the end of the second year of medical school) and summer doing autopsies. I then spent my third-year elective rotation ("free quarter") doing research in pathology, which led to my first scientific publication. I then sailed through the rest of medical school convinced I would be a pathologist, and started a pathology internship. Still, I was haunted by the thought that without taking responsibility for "live" patients I would never be a complete physician, so I decided to do a year of internal medicine—and never looked back. Unwittingly, I'd followed Osler's formula for mastering much of internal medicine: start with pathology. As an intern and resident in infectious diseases, I found that most of the patients I felt the best about, and also the patients I felt the worst about, had infections as their primary diagnoses. And I liked the cognitive aspects of infectious diseases. Whether one could make a living as an infectious diseases specialist outside of academic medical centers was highly questionable when I made this choice, but I've never regretted it. My advice: follow your interests and inclinations!

Once you have decided on medicine or surgery as an overall track, you need to choose between becoming a primary care doctor versus becoming a specialist and weigh the pros and cons. Here's what Osler said:

> **The family doctor, the private in our great army, the essential factor in the battle, should be carefully nurtured by the schools and carefully guarded by the public. Humanly speaking, with him are the issues of life and death, since upon him falls the grievous responsibility in those terrible emergencies which bring darkness and despair to so many households."**[1]

He spoke to medical students of

> **that flower of our calling—the cultivated general practitioner. May this be the destiny of a large majority of you! Have no higher ambition! You cannot reach any better position in a community; the family doctor is the man behind the gun, who does our effective work. That his life is hard and exacting; that he is underpaid and overworked; that he has but little time for study and less for recreation—these are the blows that may give finer temper to his steel, and bring out the nobler elements in his character ... Have no higher ambition than to become an all-round family doctor, whose business in life is to know disease and know how to treat it.** [2]

---

[1] On the educational value of the medical society.

[2] The student life.

If you have broad medical interests, enjoy diversity and like people, family practice may be appealing, as it was to the physician-poet William Carlos Williams (1883-1963), who enjoyed people and the practice of medicine:[3]

> It's the humdrum, day-in, day-out, everyday work that is the real satisfaction of the practice of medicine; the million and a half patients a man has seen on his daily visits over a forty-year period of week-days and Sundays that make up his life. I have never had a money practice; it would have been impossible for me. But the actual calling on people, at all times and under all conditions, the coming to grips with the intimate conditions of their lives, when they were being born, when they were dying, watching them die, watching them get well when they were ill, has always absorbed me.

For Williams, his observations during the daily practice of family medicine were grist for his literary and poetic mill. He was busy, and had to write at odd hours, like another famous physician writer and keen observer, Anton Chekhov (1860-1904), who famously remarked, "Medicine is my lawful wife and literature is my mistress; when I get fed up with one, I spend the night with the other. Though it is irregular, it is less boring this way, and besides, neither of them loses anything through my infidelity."[4] Osler too saw the appeal of general practice. Nowadays group practices lessen the isolation and financial burden of family practice.

Osler, like Williams, liked and enjoyed people. He wrote:

---

[3] Williams (1967).

[4] VanderVeer (2014).

Nothing will sustain you more potently than the power to recognize in your humdrum routine, as perhaps it may be thought, the true poetry of life—the poetry of the commonplace, of the ordinary man, of the plain toil-worn woman, with their loves and their joys, their sorrows and their griefs.[5]

This perspective of Osler might help counteract the modern tendency to spend more time ordering special tests and studies than *actually listening* to the patient's values and concerns. It also may be a key to Osler's affection for Walt Whitman, who became his patient when Osler was in Philadelphia. The patient was 65, the doctor 39.[6]

For Williams and Chekhov, the vast diversity of a general practice was part of its appeal. But in general, the broader the field encompassed by an area of medicine, the more difficult it will be to keep up. Specialists in a narrow field can stay abreast of new developments more easily, but the trade-off is the proclivity to become mere technicians. In a sense, we all become specialists because the field of medicine is far too broad for any one person to master. Osler went against the grain when he single-handedly produced an encyclopedic textbook, *The Principles and Practice of Medicine* (1892); indeed, he was the last person to do so, at least in the English language. It went through sixteen editions over 46 years and was translated into six languages. But after Osler's death in 1919, knowledge in medicine expanded far beyond any one author's ken. As early as 1881, William Pepper, whom Osler succeeded as clinical professor of medicine at Penn, asserted: "General medicine and general surgery today are federations of specialties, and the general clinician, even of the broadest gauge,

---

[5] The student life.

[6] Leon (1995).

in dealing with obscure and complicated cases, acts but as the leading partner in a medical firm."[7]

Internal medicine has indeed continued to evolve into a federation of subspecialties, with general internal medicine (its core) now being alongside other primary-care disciplines such as family practice, pediatrics, geriatrics, emergency medicine, and preventive medicine. All face the same issue: How can specialties and subspecialties best relate to the whole of medicine?[8]

In general, narrow specialties, particularly if they involve technical procedures, pay better than primary care specialties. But that is changing as payment methods evolve and fee-for-service medicine is being replaced by a more equitable system of payment. Pay-for-performance is replacing payment for procedures.[9]

AOS member Joseph J. Fins recently proposed the "creation of expert-generalists"—primary care physicians who would obtain additional training in a subspecialty area—as one way to expand access to care necessitated by increased insurance coverage under the Affordable Care Act.[10] In the present authors' opinion, this is a model well-worth exploring. In the meantime, here are some suggestions for medical students and young physicians:

- Follow your own interests and aptitudes, perhaps taking into account your temperament. If unsure, take the Myers-Briggs Test Indicator, which may help define your interests.[11]

---

[7] Pepper (1891).

[8] Bryan (2015).

[9] Chauvinism in medicine.

[10] Fins (2015).

[11] See http://www.my-personality-test.com/personality-type.

- Consult the AAMC *Careers in Medicine* website.[12]
- Approach a respected clinician or mentor and ask how they decided on a specialty. The dialogue will help clarify your thinking. Consult an authoritative source.[13]
- Become broadly conversant with most of medicine before concentrating in a relatively narrow field.
- Observe the interactions of primary care doctors and specialists, asking for yourself, "What's in this patient's best interests?"
- In referrals, make questions (to specialists) and responses (to generalists) as specific as possible.
- As you develop your own system of medical practice instigate thoughtful, unhurried primary care decisions and judicious, cost-effective referrals to specialists.

---

[12] https://www.aamc.org/cim/
[13] Freeman (2013).

THE CERTAINTY OF UNCERTAINTY

Life is short, and the Art long; the occasion fleeting; experience fallacious; and judgment difficult.
— The first aphorism of Hippocrates

Medicine, law, and theology were known as the learned professions because they were the main subjects taught in medieval universities. Their practitioners were considered learned because nearly everyone lacked higher education. (The medieval lay public was largely illiterate.) Practitioners of those professions assisted in matters of extreme importance in which the outcomes were uncertain, requiring the wise judgment of a "learned individual."

Therein rests a rub for medicine. It is difficult to imagine a world without lawyers, because the outcome of a legal contest is seldom if ever preordained. It is difficult to imagine a world without clergy because nobody knows for sure what happens to us when we die. Medicine's marriage to ever-evolving science and technology has reduced some of the uncertainty in diagnosis, treatment, and prognosis, and as a consequence, has reduced the value people place on the wise judgment of a "learned individual." Moreover, today's public is literate and can through the Internet access much scientific information. Furthermore, patients nowadays seem to want a quick fix in the form of a prescribed drug or a technological solution they have read about. (It's abetted by direct-to-consumer advertising.)

A technology-heavy style of practice explains to a large extent why health care expenditures in the U.S. (expressed as a percentage of the gross domestic product) far exceed those of any other nation, without commensurate improvements in metrics like longevity and infant mortality. Doctors and patients alike often prefer technology to talk, and the resultant cost can be measured in human terms as well as in financial terms. The quest for a quick tech-fix often overwhelms the humanistic aspect of patient care. The ethicist Stanley J. Reiser put it well: "Excessive reliance on technologies causes withdrawal of attention from personal, cultural, and social expressions of illness."[1]

The science and technology of medicine has grown by quantum leaps since Osler's day, but much of what Osler said about uncertainty and the importance of judgment still holds. He told medical students that **"Medicine is a science of uncertainty and an art of probability. . . . in taking up the study of disease, you leave the exact and certain for the inexact and doubtful and enter a realm in which to a great extent the certainties are replaced by probabilities. . . . The practice of medicine is an art, based on science."[2]**

Osler's thoughts were echoed in a 2016 article[3] in the NEJM titled "Tolerating Uncertainty—The Next Medical Revolution?" in which the authors stated

> "Key elements for survival in the medical profession would seem, intuitively, to be a tolerance for uncertainty and a curiosity about the unknown. Have we created

[1] Reiser (2009).

[2] Bean (1950).

[3] Simpkin and Schwartzstein (2016).

a culture that ignores that requirement? Could our intolerance of uncertainty, in turn, be contributing to the accelerating rates of burnout and the rising cost of health care? For there is no doubt that absolute truth and certainty are hard to come by in clinical medicine."

But due to the variability in disease and in humans, the science is inexact, lacking the certainty of, say, physics or mathematics. In 1963 the Johns Hopkins psychiatrist John C. Whitehorn[4] described medical education as "education for uncertainty." Trained as a scientist, Whitehorn confessed that he, like most people, was "personally and temperamentally . . . opposed to uncertainty," yet, he writes, "whoever as a physician takes the responsibility for the clinical judgment and for the guidance of living human beings" must develop "knowledge of human nature and some skill in the leadership of real living persons." In this regard, "the educated physician" has distinct advantages over the "technically trained physician" who lacks a liberal education. Whitehorn called for "better humanization of medical education" and better teaching in the sciences with more emphasis on the limitations of knowledge. We agree.

Despite our panoply of impressive technologies, important decisions in medicine still require judgment more often than not. By some estimates only about 20% to 30% of what doctors do is predicated on results of first-rate studies, hence the strong emphasis today on evidence-based practice. Neuroscientists now are studying how our brains respond to uncertainty: the brain can be conceptualized as a probability machine that constantly makes predictions about the world and updates them based on what it receives from the senses. They are studying how uncon-

---

[4] Whitehorn (1963).

scious influences affect our decision making, how people differ in their ability to tolerate uncertainty, how stress affects our ability to make wise decisions in the context of uncertainty, and how, through "complexity science" we might improve health care delivery systems.[5]

Probabilities and uncertainties are worth keeping in the forefront of our thinking. As director of an emergency department (ED) JBV recalls reviewing the care of a 25-year-old-man complaining of chest pain after taking a spill water skiing. The physician who saw the patient in the ED was thinking of a traumatic cause, and when, on physical exam, there were rales in the chest, he added water inhalation as an additional cause for the chest pain. The doctor did not consider a myocardial infarction (MI) as a diagnosis because the patient's age made it improbable. The patient was treated and discharged home. It was a lethal mistake, and illustrated Hippocrates first aphorism.

The patient returned the next day in florid congestive failure, went rapidly downhill and died before any intervention could occur. Although an original diagnosis of MI was improbable, it was still *possible,* and was *potentially lethal*, and should have been ruled out at the first visit. MI turned out to be the diagnosis, proved at autopsy. Additional history (obtained post mortem, which <u>could</u> have been brought out at the first visit) revealed that *the patient had a twin brother who had died of cardiac disease,* which would have been highly significant, had it been elicited by the doctor.

Twenty-first century advances will reduce many present-day uncertainties in medical practice, but new areas of uncertainty will doubtless appear. In the meantime, here are some suggestions for fellow learners:

---

[5] Leykum et al (2014).

- Be humble about what you know, and about what you think you know. Osler wrote, **"The greater the ignorance, the greater the dogmatism."**[6] He reminisced to students and faculty at McGill 25 years after his initial faculty appointment there, that **"I have learned since to be a better student, and to be ready to say to my fellow students, 'I do not know.'"**[7]

- Resist the pressure to make absolute diagnoses, leaving open the possibility that a problem might have another explanation. Osler reportedly said: **"Absolute diagnoses are unsafe, and are made at the expense of the conscience."** It is true that newer laboratory tests, newer approaches to securing tissue diagnoses and especially an array of imaging methods that would astound Osler, often allow absolute diagnoses. And true, the business aspects of medicine such as coding and billing practices often demand absolute diagnoses. However, we strongly encourage that your notes reflect at least a hint of uncertainty.

- Reflect. Develop the habit of "reflective practice," looking back on what you did and what you might do differently and make notes in a day-journal or in this *vade mecum*. "The best doctors," CSB learned from a mentor, "think about their patients in the shower." Osler noted: **"Various degrees of probability we may attain to and do reach daily but in the busy round of teaching and practice we are apt to forget that positive certainty until we have a rude awakening and a useful lesson in the folly of over-confidence."**[8]

---

[6] Chauvinism in medicine.

[7] After twenty-five years.

[8] Chauvinism in medicine.

- Base your decisions on the clinical context, which includes the best evidence-based information (ideally including a meticulous history and physical examination, knowledge of the medical literature, and a careful review of the differential diagnosis, including "the worst thing that might be wrong with the patient—as in the ED example above).

- Observe the decision-making styles of those around you. Form private opinions about the extent to which their use of technology (including therapeutics) seems evidence-based, cost-effective and rational (reflecting wise judgment). Learn from observing your peers.

- Observe the extent to which those around you sometimes order tests and procedures primarily for the sake of "defensive medicine." Form an opinion about whether such practices might be reduced by encouraging the habit of writing a few sentences about why, in your judgment, this or that test or procedure does not seem cost effective, using such concepts as NNT (the number of patients that would need to be tested to produce a single positive, clinically-relevant result).

- Encourage shared decision-making. Especially when there are multiple ways to approach diagnosis and therapy, present the options for the patient (or patient's surrogate), and don't insist on the final say.

- Finally, evaluate your own tolerance for uncertainty, including the extent to which uncertainty makes you anxious and/or depressed compared to your peers. Osler observed: **"In differing degrees differing with our temperaments, there come upon us bouts of depression . . . the worries of heart to which we doctors are so subject make us feel bitterly the uncertainties**

of medicine as a profession, and at times make us despair of its future." [9]

Don't be afraid to share your concerns with a senior mentor. And always keep in the back of your mind that first aphorism of Hippocrates!

---

[9] Elisha Bartlett.

MENTORS AND MENTORING

Mentoring historically is a huge part of medical education, which for most of recorded history has been an apprentice system. It still persists in the environment of residency training, where senior physicians take their juniors under wing and often serve as role models for them. In general terms, a mentor is anyone who provides knowledge, advice, counsel, support, and opportunity in such a way as to help a protégé's pursuit of full membership in a profession. Throughout life, from student days, through residency and into practice years, we learn from mentors; the need is life-long.[1] A help-seeking medical student will recognize many mentors ranging from classmates (peer mentors) to senior professors. Mentoring can be formal (as by scheduled appointments) or informal (as by "curbside" advice). One of the authors, while in the doldrums of trying to master gross anatomy in the library, was invited by an intern he did not know to spend an evening in the emergency department. It gave a refreshing infusion of clinical medicine and was a splendid example of mentoring, early on.

Osler enjoyed a series of mentors throughout his life. Father William Arthur Johnson, founder and warden of Trinity College School in Weston, Ontario, taught him microscopy, stimulated his

---

[1] Johnson and Ridley (2004).

interest in the natural sciences, and acquainted him with the writings of Sir Thomas Browne. Johnson inspired Osler's lifelong pursuit of both the sciences and the humanities. Dr. James Bovell, an eccentric physician in whose residence Osler spent the winter of 1869-1870, reinforced those dual interests and helped him decide on a medical career instead of pursuing the cloth (as his father had).

Osler more or less "fell into" mentoring relationships with Johnson and Bovell, but as a medical student he actively sought out Dr. Palmer Howard, a stern man most students found hard to approach. The story goes that Osler went to Howard's house late one night to clarify a point Howard had made in a lecture earlier that day. Howard didn't have a ready answer, and the two were soon poring over books. Howard invited Osler to return, and came to regard Osler almost as a son. Here we find a lesson: Many older people, while seemingly aloof, will welcome a younger person who seriously and sincerely asks for advice. Osler overcame fears (known to salespersons as "call reluctance") and approached Howard with a *specific* question. Why not follow Osler's example? Identify a potential mentor, one whose personality might mesh well with yours (a similar sense of humor helps). Many older people take great pride in discovering and helping a future star!

The seventeenth-century English physician, Sir Thomas Browne, became a life-long mentor for Osler. (See also section on FAITH.) Browne's *Religio Medici* (1642) became the touchstone for Osler's inner life. Indeed, at his funeral, it lay on top of his coffin in the chapel of Christ Church College, Oxford, on New Year's Day, 1920. Osler called the *Religio* "the most precious book in my library" and told students:

From such books come subtle influences which give stability to character and help to give a man

a sane outlook on the complex problems of life. . . . Mastery of self, conscientious devotion to duty, deep human interest in human beings—these best of all lessons you must learn now or never; and these are some of the lessons which may be gleaned from the writings of Sir Thomas Browne.[2]

Summing up Browne's impact on his life, Osler mentioned

[There are] three lessons to be gathered from the life of Sir Thomas Browne, all of them of value to-day. First, we see in him a man who had an ideal education . . . . The second important lesson we may gain is that he presents a remarkable example in the medical profession of a man who mingled the waters of science with the oil of faith . . . The third lesson to be drawn is that the perfect life may be led in a very simple, quiet way.[3]

Osler during his mature years had few intense mentor-protégé relationships but was always eager to help students and younger colleagues to the extent that he was known as "the young man's friend." When as a young faculty member he was asked to give an introductory lecture to medical students, he told them: **"You come now into the society not of mere professors, who will lecture you at a distance, but of men who are anxious for your welfare, who will sympathize with your difficulties and also bear with your weaknesses. . . . Look upon us as elder brothers to whom you can come confidently and fearlessly for advice in any trouble or difficulty."** He took the attitude that

[2] Sir Thomas Browne.
[3] Cushing (1925), ii, 24-5.

we are all fellow students. In a lecture on "The Student Life," he anticipated the trend for education to become much more "democratic" than was formerly the case:

> **The successful teacher is no longer on a height, pumping knowledge at high pressure into passive receptacles. The new methods have changed all this. He is no longer *Sir Oracle*, perhaps unconsciously by his very manner antagonizing minds to whose level he cannot possibly descend, but he is a senior student anxious to help his juniors. When a simple, earnest spirit animates a college, there is no appreciable interval between the teacher and the taught—both are in the same class, the one a little more advanced than the other. So animated, the student feels that he has joined a family whose honor, whose welfare is his own, and whose interests should be his first consideration.[4]**

Osler illustrated the ideal mentoring relationship when he gave *"latch-keys"* (allowing 24-hour access to his home and library) to certain young physicians at Johns Hopkins. One of them, Harvey Cushing, came to know him well and later wrote Osler's two-volume biography.[5]

The digital revolution's democratization of medical knowledge now levels the playing field between the most senior professor and the most junior student to an extent that Osler would have found unimaginable. The potential for rich relationships between mentors and their protégés (mentees) is thus brighter than ever in the Internet age!

---

[4] The student life.
[5] Cushing (1925).

Mentoring is a two-way street. It requires someone willing to teach and someone willing to learn. How do you pick a mentor? Some aspects we have noted are:

- Admiration—someone you want to emulate.
- A special skill or ability you want to acquire.
- A resonance with your own personality (it helps if you find the same things funny!).
- Fit into your mentor's schedule—don't expect it the other-way-around. The future physician-writer Robert Coles[6] admired the poet-physician William Carlos Williams and chose to write his undergraduate Harvard senior thesis about him; he shadowed him in his practice and established a mentoring relationship which immensely enriched Coles' life when he later became a physician.
- Be willing to <u>work</u> <u>hard</u> (recall Osler's master-word— **work**!). In the educational hierarchy of medicine, rewards come with hard work.

JBV had an instructive experience as a surgical resident. Coming on to a new three-month rotation with three downtown surgeons, I asked Bill, the resident coming off service, what he'd gotten to do. "S--t," he replied. "I didn't get to do anything but some assisting." Later that day I ran into the junior surgeon in the downtown partnership in the hall at the University. "You want to do some surgery?" he said. "Then don't be like that lazy SOB, Bill. Get down early and see our patients before we go to surgery and give us a report." That's all he said, but I took it to heart and early Monday morning went to the downtown hospital ward and made quick rounds on their five patients with the night nurse. A

---

[6] Cox (2005).

few minutes later as I was scrubbing my hands with the senior surgeon, Dr. B., he asked about his three patients, and I gave him a brief report.

The patient being put to sleep was a slender woman with ulcer disease. I'd never done the planned operation (a gastrectomy)— I'd not even <u>seen</u> one done—but I'd read up on it the previous night. The surgeon was given the knife by the scrub nurse. He looked at the anesthesiologist, who nodded to go ahead. Then Dr. B. reached over and handed me the knife, saying, "Joe, why don't you do this one." He gracefully and gently led me through the operation. I was scared, but exhilarated. I did a lot more surgery on that rotation, and I had three excellent mentors for the next three months!

FOUR APPENDICES

APPENDIX A

WHO WAS WILLIAM OSLER?
WHY IS HE IMPORTANT?
WHAT WOULD HE DO IF ALIVE TODAY?

In the spring of 2016, MEDSCAPE, the online resource for physicians and other health care professionals, polled U.S. doctors in order to rank "the most influential physicians" of all time. Sir William Osler (1849-1919) topped the list. This begs the question, "What was special about Osler?"

"William Osler is the quintessential physician of our time because of his literary legacy, scientific and clinical accomplishments, educational contributions, and influence on professional relations. He had an extraordinary personality, a facile wit, a bibliographic spirit, and a philosophy of life that permitted him to envision and achieve remarkable goals. Osler's humanism, which permeated all of his activities, was the sine qua non of his particular claim to posterity . . . The life and philosophy of William Osler continues to serve as a standard of excellence and a model for the evolution of the profession and its practitioners." This passage comes from the late AOS member Richard L. Golden's preface to *The Quotable Osler*,[1] which contains over 800 excerpts from Osler's writings and sayings.

---

[1] Silverman et al (2003), xxxii.

Osler was born in 1849, the youngest son of an Anglican priest in what is now Ontario. His mother, who lived to be 100, was said to be as familiar with the scriptures as her husband, and William's later familiarity with the Bible had its roots in his family. In his early education he was headed for the cloth, but early on one of his school headmasters sparked an interest in science. He went to the University of Toronto and studied theology for a year, but—under the influence of a second mentor—chose medicine. Osler later dedicated his textbook to his three early mentors (Table).

Table 1. SIR WILLIAM OSLER: CHRONOLOGY	
1849	Born July 12 at Bond Head Parsonage in Tecumseth Township, Upper Canada, the eighth child and young-est son of an Anglican priest who had immigrated to Canada from Cornwall, England.
1867-1868	Mentored by Father W. A. Johnson, a parish priest in Weston, Ontario, who interested him in both the sciences (especially through microscopy) and in the humanities.
1868-1870	Mentored by James Bovell, a physician in Toronto; chose a career in medicine over a career in the clergy.
1871-1872	Mentored by R. Palmer Howard, a physician in Mon-treal; encouraged to study "all of medicine"; received M.D. from McGill University.
1872-1874	Studied medicine in London, Berlin, and Vienna; resolved to become a generalist-consultant physician "of the first rank."
1874-1884	Taught and practiced at McGill University and at Montreal General Hospital; performed about 1,000 autopsies; rose through the academic ranks.

1884-1889	Served as professor of clinical medicine at the University of Pennsylvania; word spread of his prowess at medicine and at teaching.
1889-1905	Served as the first professor of medicine at the Johns Hopkins University School of Medicine; delivered a number of inspirational addresses, some of which were eventually published as *Aequanimitas With Other Addresses to Medical Students, Nurses and Practitioners of Medicine.*
1892	Completed *The Principles and Practice of Medicine*, a comprehensive textbook that quickly became the standard in the English-speaking world; he married Grace Linzee Revere Gross, the widow of Philadelphia surgeon Samuel W. Gross; the couple had been friends of Osler.
1905-1919	Served as Regius Professor of Medicine at Oxford University.
1911	Made a baronet as part of the coronation honors of George V, and thus became *Sir* William Osler.
1917	Death of his only surviving child, Edward Revere Osler, who was killed in Flanders (Belgium) by a German artillery shell.
1919	Delivered "The Old Humanities and the New Science," his last major address. Died December 29 at age 70 of complications of pneumonia.

Osler began medical school in Toronto, then switched to McGill, and after graduation in 1872 (age 23) he studied in Europe before returning to join the faculty at McGill. There he remained ten years, did about 1,000 autopsies, and became an accomplished lecturer. He was called to join the faculty at Penn where he remained five years and then was invited to become professor of medicine at the new medical school in Baltimore that had been funded by the will of the Quaker merchant Johns Hopkins. There, after the hospital had opened but before the medical school was operational, he completed his textbook. He was 43.

He had proposed to the widow Gross (as he affectionately teased her) before he left Philadelphia, but using a cobbler's phrase, she told him to "stick to his last" and finish the textbook. She became the recipient of the first copy when he put it on her lap, saying, "Here, take the darn thing; now what are you going to do with the man?"[2] They were married soon thereafter, and she—

William and Grace Osler

[2] Cushing (1925), i, 357-8.

descended from the Reveres of Boston—became a perfect fit as a wife, being socially adept, often hosting meals for his students and colleagues during their next twenty-six years together.

In addition to *The Principles and Practice of Medicine*, which established his reputation, Osler delivered a number of inspirational addresses punctuated with many allusions to the classics and the scriptures, later published as *Aequanimitas With other Addresses*. (In 2001, Shigeaki Hinohara and Hisae Niki, a Japanese physician and a professor of English, respectively, published a collection of Osler's essays that extensively annotates Osler's many references and literary allusions. Reading *Osler's A Way of Life and Other Addresses with Commentary and Annotations*[3] is an excellent way for today's students to become familiar with Osler's inspirational writings.)

Osler spent 16 years at Johns Hopkins, where he taught alongside his famous colleagues William Welch (pathology), William Stewart Halsted (surgery), and Howard A. Kelly (gynecology), captured in John Singer Sargent's famous painting *The Four Doctors* (1905). Over those years, in addition to a full schedule of teaching and writing, he was called on to see increasing numbers of patients in consultation. It was an exhausting schedule. When an offer came to become the Regius Professor of Medicine at Oxford, he and Grace, with their ten-year-old son Revere, made the move.

Revere became the light of his father's life, enrolled in Oxford, and when the Great War (World War I) broke out, joined the army, serving in an artillery unit in Flanders. On August 29, 1918, his unit received a direct hit. Revere did not survive his abdominal and chest wounds, despite the ministrations of American surgeons Harvey Cushing and George Crile, both of whom were friends

---

[3] Hinohara and Niki (2001).

of his father. Although some historians postulate that Osler died of depression resulting from his son's death, the most recent biographer, Michael Bliss,[4] rejects this idea. Bliss feels that he died simply of complications of pneumonia, which Osler had sometimes called "the old man's friend."

Osler's ashes and those of his widow, Lady Grace Osler, now reside in the Osler library of the History of Medicine at McGill, which also houses most of Osler's own library of over 7,000 volumes (the *Bibliotheca Osleriana*) that he bequeathed to his alma mater.

On May 2, 1905, as Osler was about to leave America to sail for England and a new career at Oxford, more than 500 leaders of the North American medical profession assembled in the grand ballroom of New York's Waldorf-Astoria Hotel to bid him farewell. Osler profusely thanked his many friends, and then, for the first time, enumerated his personal ideals:[5]

> **I have had three personal ideals. One is to do the day's work well and not to bother about tomorrow.... The second ideal has been to act the Golden Rule, as far as in me lay, towards my professional brethren and towards the patients committed to my care. And the third ideal has been to cultivate such a measure of equanimity as would enable me to bear success with humility, the affection of my friends without pride, and to be ready when the day of sorrow and grief came to meet it with the courage befitting a man.**

---

[4] Bliss (1999), 473.
[5] L'Envoi.

How should we regard Osler's ideals? Although he apparently listed his ideals only on that one occasion, he encouraged students to be idealists. We concur and feature Osler's three ideals twice in this *vade mecum* because we believe they are still valid and worthy of emulation today. Not that we invariably live up to the highest ideals—we are men and women, fallible as humans are—but holding ideals helps nurture and fan the flame of altruism, so important in the life of the caring physician. We share Osler's optimism for the future of medicine, and his humanistic conviction that **"we are here not to get all we can out of life for ourselves, but to try to make the lives of others happier."**[6]

Our answer to the question **"What would Osler do were he alive today?"** is simple. He could not solve all our complex problems, but we could profit from his ability to inspire.

Osler's most enduring legacy for us remains his ideals, his optimism, and his hope that medicine might be mankind's best hope for a peaceful and durable future.[7] He is the subject of over 2,000 articles in peer-reviewed journals and two excellent biographies, a recent one by Michael Bliss[8] and an earlier, Pulitzer Prize-winning one by Harvey Cushing.[9] Osler was an exemplary physician and teacher but he was not the flawless saint humorously portrayed in the cartoon by *Max Brödel* (see next page). We should study Osler the same way we study all potential role models, past and present: namely observe, make notes, and try to internalize his better qualities. Osler would want it that way. He would want us to enjoy our practices, our patients, our colleagues, and our profession.

---

[6] The master-word in medicine.
[7] Inlow (1964); Bryan (1999).
[8] Bliss (1999).
[9] Cushing (1925).

In 1896 the medical illustrator Max Brödel portrayed Osler as "The Saint," hovering over the Johns Hopkins Hospital. Infectious pathogens flee the Osler cyclone. Many and perhaps most of Osler's contemporaries praised Osler for his uncommonly humanistic qualities. However he, like us, had his shortcomings and foibles.

APPENDIX B

THE AMERICAN OSLER SOCIETY (AOS)

This manual for millennial medical students and residents is sponsored and published by the American Osler Society (AOS), a national society whose members are dedicated to preserve and promulgate the memory, values and teachings of Sir William Osler, who lived from 1849 to 1919. (Details of his life and career are given in Appendix A.) At age 43, Osler was the single author of one of the outstanding textbooks of medicine, which went through sixteen editions and was translated into six foreign languages.

Medical science always moves on and Osler's textbook (*The Practice of Medicine*) is out of date, supplanted by a variety of multi-authored textbooks. But its early editions stimulated John D. Rockefeller to set up the Rockefeller Foundation for Medical Research in 1901 and the Rockefeller Institute in 1913. Osler also wrote many essays and addresses, some of which are still relevant for today's students and residents. Several of these are cited in the reference list at the end of this volume. We have quoted Osler extensively throughout this work.

This small volume is not a handbook about the scientific practice of medicine, nor is it an ethics manual, though it contains a framework for ethical reflection and decision-making. The Science of Medicine is ever enlarging and changing; the Art of Medicine has changed more slowly; its components relate to humanism and historical aspects of its past. William Osler still speaks cogently to the enduring aspects of the Art of the practice of medicine.

The AOS is a group of about two hundred physicians and historians that meets annually, usually in a city in North America, but occasionally abroad. At its annual meetings the AOS features papers about Osler, the humanities in medical practice, and the history of medicine. (See the AOS website <www.americanosler. org> for more information about the Society, its Annual Meeting, and the Bean competition). Medical students are encouraged to attend, with expenses paid for the winners of a special award named after the first AOS president, William Bean, who had been professor of medicine at Iowa.

Emerson famously said **"Books are for the scholar's idle time,"** meaning the student should study nature rather than read others' works. In a similar vein, Osler offered a pithy aphorism: **"To study the phenomena of disease without books is to sail an uncharted sea, while to study books without patients is not to go to sea at all."**[1] The authors of this *vade mecum* believe our patients are the greatest source of our education, and to that end, this volume has blank pages for jotting down notes about patients you work up. Even better, we recommend that every medical student purchase a blank journal. In it record interesting observations, quotes, patient stories and lessons learned. Osler urged students to **"carry a small notebook which will fit into your pocket and never ask a new patient a question without it."**[2] Getting to know our patients and caring for them are two of the greatest joys of medical practice.

---

[1] Books and men.
[2] The student life.

There have been enormous changes in the *Science* of medicine since Osler's day: Think of just six of them: antibiotics and chemotherapy, CAT and PET scans, organ transplantation and joint replacement. There are dozens of others. The ever-broadening base of knowledge and techniques has spawned a plethora of specialties, because each of us can embrace and master only a small fraction of what is known and valuable to treat human illness. The vast expansion of knowledge in all fields of medicine means there are scores of textbooks—a comprehensive textbook by a single author, such as Osler's would be impossible today. But today Osler would keep up within the field of medicine he chose, all through his professional life, just as physicians today must keep up.

Keeping up with the *Science* of Medicine requires commitment to life-long learning, to staying abreast of the constantly expanding body of skills and knowledge, through courses and meetings, on-line updates, journal reading and interaction with colleagues. It's part of staying competent in one's chosen field.

Maintaining one's idealism and altruism—what we might call keeping up with the *Art* of Medicine—means stoking the inner fire that led us to choose a career in medicine in the first place. That too means commitment, but of a different sort, done differently by each of us. We believe that commitment to the *Art* is every bit as important as commitment to the *Science* of medicine and surgery. But it's harder, because of the press of time and the inexorable expansion of technology. That's where the ideals, counsel, and example of William Osler are relevant. For example, consider what Osler called his three ideals,[3] (cited in Appendix A) which are excellent advice to physicians today, whatever their background or religious persuasion.

---

[3] L'Envoi.

Moreover, we in the AOS have abstracted advice from his writings and believe it offers much for today's physicians. Consider the following, which we might classify as additional "Oslerian" ideals:

- ***Read something non-medical*** at the end of the day or first thing in the morning. Osler urged us to **"have a book open on your dressing table."** He suggested a bedside library of ten volumes[4] to help round out the scientific education of the physician, a list that included the Bible, the Works of Shakespeare, Emerson, O. W. Holmes and several ancient authors rarely read nowadays. We have devoted Appendix C to the subject of a bedside library for today's student.

- ***Be charitable***—give away your coat, as Osler did on a cold wintry day, as witnessed by his niece in Montreal in 1872, when he gave it to a poorly clad beggar. Within a fortnight, as he was dying, the man returned the coat and willed Osler his hob-nail liver.[5]

- ***Be magnanimous***—Osler continually encouraged his colleagues, students and residents, in person and by letter or brief card. He even supplied their needs out of his own pocket, when on the faculty at McGill he purchased microscopes for the class when he introduced the institution's first course in physiology and histology.[6]

- ***Listen to the patient***—who is telling you the diagnosis. Knowing the patient is just as important as knowing the disease. Osler urged students at the Albany Medical

---

[4] Bedside library for medical students.

[5] Abbott M (1926), 172-3.

[6] Cushing H (1925).

College,[7] **"Care more particularly for the individual patient than for the special features of the disease."** Every disease we are called to treat comes to us as part of a unique person, and is affected by their worries and cares.

- *Exercise your heart as well as your head* as you care for your patients **"The practice of medicine is an art, not a trade; a calling, not a business; a calling in which your heart will be exercised equally with your head.**[8] As physicians and surgeons we are called to be more than mere technicians.

- *See in your daily routine the true poetry of life*. Osler advised **"Nothing will sustain you more potently than the power to recognize in your humdrum routine, as perhaps it may be thought, the true poetry of life—the poetry of the commonplace, of the ordinary man, of the plain toll-worn woman, with their loves and their joys, their sorrows and their griefs."**[9] This perspective of Osler would help counteract the modern tendency to spend more time ordering special tests and studies than *actually listening* to the patient's values and concerns. It also may be a key to Osler's affection for Walt Whitman, who became his patient when Osler was in Philadelphia. The patient was 65, the doctor 39.[10]

- *Have a systematic approach to knowledge and to life*. **"The secret of successful working lies in the systematic arrangement of what you have to do, and in the methodical performance of it. With all of you**

---

[7] Osler W (1899). Address to the students of the Albany Medical College.

[8] The master-word in medicine.

[9] The student life.

[10] Leon, PW (1995), 21.

this is possible, for few disturbing elements exist in the student's life to interrupt the allotted duty which each hour of the day should possess. Make out, each one for himself, a time-table, with the hours of lecture, study, and recreation, and follow closely and conscientiously the program there indicated. I know of no better way to accomplish a large amount of work, and it saves the mental worry and anxiety which will surely haunt you if your tasks are done in an irregular and desultory way."[11] Osler husbanded his time with care, often catching up on journal reading on the train en route to a consultation or a medical meeting. We believe that he would admit that a smart phone can promote system; but would warn that it can become a great distraction.

- *Get involved in a medical society*—as a corrective. Osler wrote: **"No class of men need friction so much as physicians; no class gets less. The daily round of a busy practitioner tends to develop an egoism of a most intense kind, to which there is no antidote. The few set-backs are forgotten. The mistakes are often buried, and ten years of successful work tends to make a man touchy, dogmatic, intolerant of correction and abominably self centered. To this mental attitude the medical society is the best corrective, and a man misses a good part of his education who does not get knocked about a bit by his colleagues in discussions and criticisms."**[12] (A surgical morbidity and mortality conference also can serve a similar purpose.)

---

[11] Osler W (1877). Introductory Lecture, 11.
[12] Osler W (1897). The function of a state faculty.

- *Be observant and publish your observations.* **"When you have made and recorded the unusual or original observation, or when you have accomplished a piece of research in laboratory or ward, do not be satisfied with a verbal communication at a medical society. Publish it."**[13] Writing papers requires effort, but is rewarding and satisfying. Jotting notes in this *vade mecum* is a great way to later recall interesting cases and particular lessons learned from your patients.

- *Keep your sense of humor.* **"Hilarity and humor, a breezy cheerfulness, a nature "sloping toward the sunny side," as Lowell has it, help enormously both in the study and the practice of medicine. To many of a sombre and sour disposition it is hard to maintain good spirits amid the trials and tribulations of the day, and yet it is an unpardonable mistake to go about among patients with a long face."**[14] Osler brought healing and cheerfulness to the patient's bedside.

Osler was what we would call an upbeat person. Throughout his life, he enjoyed practical jokes, whether as a boy (as when he whispered in turn to his father, then to a visitor, that "you'll have to speak loudly—he's nearly deaf."[15]), or as an adult, when he explained to his colleague William McCallum how a banquet entrée was prepared. Osler made up a tall tale about how the serving of scrod (a culinary term for a young codfish that has been split and boned) had been prepared, telling the gullible pathologist that scrod was a castrated fish, just like a capon was a cas-

---

[13] Thayer, WS. (1969). Osler the teacher.

[14] The student life.

[15] Bryan (1997). In the opinion of JBV, Bryan's book is the best source for relating Osler's life and example to current medical practice.

trated rooster.[16] The epitome of Osler's puckish humor occurred under the pseudonym Egerton Yorrick Davis.[17] Those papers by his alter ego are worth reading today and still elicit a smile. Yet he was well aware of the tragic side of life and his disposition helped lift the burden of illness in his patients.

All of the above were important facets of Osler's life that we can incorporate into ours. The authors, as members of the American Osler Society, believe that the just and charitable life, the intellectual resourcefulness, and the ethical example of Sir William Osler are worthy of emulation by students and practicing physicians. His ideals and values can help us all practice the **Art** and **Science** of medicine with renewed vigor.

---

[16] Pratt JH (1949).
[17] Nation, EF (1969).

APPENDIX C

A BEDSIDE LIBRARY

In the Ingersoll Lecture at Harvard in 1904 Osler wrote **"The man of science is in a sad quandary today. He cannot but feel that the emotional side to which faith leans makes for all that is bright and joyous in life. Fed on the dry husks of facts, the human heart has a hidden want which science cannot supply; as a steady diet it is too strong and meaty, and hinders rather than promotes harmonious mental metabolism."**[1]

Rare is the medical student who has not become parched with the steady diet of scientific facts he must master each day. Osler suggested a remedy that he called a bedside library for medical students, which he set forth on the last page of *Aequanimitas,* the book of his collected essays. He maintained that by reading for one half hour before going to sleep, one could **"get the education, if not of a scholar, at least of a gentleman. Before going to sleep read for half an hour, and in the morning have a book open on your dressing table. You will be surprised to find how much can be accomplished in the course of a year."**[2]

---

[1] Science and Immortality, 42.

[2] Aequanimitas, (an unnumbered page that follows page 452 in this work).

Osler's bedside library was a list of ten books, some still well known, like the Bible and Shakespeare, plus others not familiar to today's medical students. Contemporary physician-poet Jack Coulehan has this comment about Osler's list:

It was a list well-tailored to his own beliefs and personality. Osler's philosophy of life was largely a Christian version of the classical Stoic philosophy, as presented by Epictetus (*Discourses*) and Marcus Aurelius (*Meditations*). Emerson's essays and Plutarch's *Lives* spoke to Osler's ethic of virtue and character formation, while Montaigne provided a model of introspection and personal reflection. He believed a careful reading of Shakespeare could illustrate the complexity, depth, drama, and comedy of human character. Cervantes' *Don Quixote* stimulated the moral imagination while Oliver Wendell Holmes' stories offered more homely medical anecdotes and wisdom. In *Religio Medici*, the 17th century physician Sir Thomas Browne sets forth "a doctor's religion." While modern readers can be put off by his grandiloquent style and primitive science, I imagine Osler wanted his students to focus on Browne's deep human sensitivity and surprisingly modern religious tolerance.[3]

We strongly endorse the concept of a bedside library, but would suggest some other books for today's medical students. In 2010, the American College of Physicians published a book edited by Drs. Michael LaCombe and David Elpern, titled *Osler's Bedside Library: Great Writers Who Inspired a Great Physician*

---

[3] Coulehan J (2016).

(which discusses 33 works).[4] It gives background information for Osler's list of ten plus 23 other books that modern physicians have suggested as an updated bedside library. Several other lists have also been proposed. [5, 6]

Contemporary medical students have much more scientific information to master than students in Osler's day. What's needed as a counterbalance to the lopsided scientific academic load is a list of books that if regularly read will help fan the coals of student idealism into a flame that won't be quenched by the scientific onslaught. Here are ten of our favorite bedside books (the first two also led Osler's list). We encourage students to fill their own bedside library shelf.

1. *The Guideposts Parallel Bible* (1981) presents in parallel four versions of the Old and the New Testaments.[7]
2. *The Complete Works of Shakespeare*, (an Oxford Edition) is also a good reference work.
3. *On Doctoring: Stories, Poems, Essays* (3d Ed, 2001) by R. Reynolds and J. Stone. This volume contains some of the best "modern" writing pertaining to the art of practicing medicine.
4. *The Physician in Literature* (1982) edited by Norman Cousins. Works by and about physicians in history.
5. *Osler: Inspirations from a Great Physician* (1997) by C. Bryan. If you had to pick one book to learn more about Osler, this would be it. (JBV's opinion)

---

[4] Lacombe M, Elpern D (2010).

[5] Murray J (2009).

[6] Liveanu A (2009).

[7] These are The King James, the Revised Standard, the New International and the Living Bible versions.

6. *Osler's 'A Way of Life' & Other Addresses, with Commentary* (2001) by Hinohara and Niki gives extensive notes about the many classical and Biblical allusions used by Osler.

7. *The Call of Stories: Teaching and the Moral Imagination* (1989) by R. Coles presents the allure of stories by an excellent physician teacher.

8. *Man's Search for Meaning* (1946) by V. Frankl is a classic in understanding the three common characteristics that enabled those who survived Auschwitz, applicable to everyone today.

9. *Advice to the Healer: On the Art of Caring* (2012) by R. Colgan includes good, short biographies of medical luminaries like Nightingale, Osler, Schweitzer, Peabody and Pellegrino, plus much practical advice.

10. *The Little, Brown Book of Anecdotes* (1985) Ed. by Clifton Fadiman. A collection of hundreds of anecdotes that can add inspiration and even levity at the start or the end of a busy day.

APPENDIX D

THE MODERNIZED AMA CODE OF MEDICAL ETHICS

At the Annual meeting of the American Medical Association (AMA) in June 2016, a comprehensive update of the *Code of Medical Ethics* was adopted. In a "Viewpoint" article[1] (side bar box) the Principles of Medical Ethics were summarized, which we reproduce here.

1. A physician shall be dedicated to providing competent medical care with compassion and respect for human dignity and rights.
2. A physician shall uphold the standards of professionalism, be honest in all professional interactions, and strive to report physicians deficient in character or competence, or engaging in fraud or deception, to appropriate entities.
3. A physician shall respect the law and also recognize a responsibility to seek changes in those requirements which are to the best interests of patients.
4. A physician shall respect the rights of patients, colleagues, and other health professionals, and shall

---

[1] Brotherton S et al (2016).

safeguard patient confidences within the constraints of the law.

5. A physician shall continue to study, apply and advance scientific knowledge, maintain a commitment to medical education, make relevant information available to patients, colleagues and the public, obtain consultation, and use the talents of other health professionals when indicated.

6. A physician shall, in the provision of appropriate patient care, except in emergencies, be free to choose whom to serve, with whom to associate, and the environment in which to provide medical care.

7. A physician shall recognize a responsibility to participate in activities contributing to the improvement of the community and the betterment of public health.

8. A physician shall, while caring for a patient, regard responsibility to the patient as paramount.

9. A physician shall support access to medical care for all people.

BIBLIOGRAPHY

Note: *In the chapter footnote citations, Osler's **essays** contained in his 1932 monograph* Aequanimitas With other Addresses to Medical Students, Nurses, and Practitioners in Medicine (3rd edition) ***are cited by title only.*** *All his other writings— as with other authors' works—are cited by name and date of publication.*

Abbott ME ed. (1926). Sir William Osler Memorial Number. *Bulletin No. IX of the International Association of Medical Museums and Journal of Technical Methods.* Montreal, Canada: Privately issued.

Alessandra T, O'Connor MJ (1996). *The Platinum Rule: Discover the Four Basic Business Personalities and How They Can Lead You to Success.* New York: Business Plus.

Andre C (2015). *Looking at Mindfulness: 25 Ways to Live in the Moment through Art.* New York: Blue Rider Press.

Arnold P. Gold Foundation (2016) see http://www.gold-foundation.org /about-us/faqs/

Asher R (1972). *Richard Asher Talking Sense.* Baltimore: University Park Press.

Baltes PB, Smith J (1990). Toward a psychology of wisdom and its ontogenesis. In: Sternberg RJ, ed. *Wisdom: Its*

Nature, Origins, and Development. Cambridge: Cambridge University Press; 1990: 87-120.

Barker LF (1926). Dr. Osler as the young physician's friend and exemplar. In: *Abbott* (1926): 251-8.

Bebell LM (2016). Cough it up: a health care paradox. *JAMA* 317: 1149-50.

Bean WB, ed. (1968). *Sir William Osler: Aphorisms from his Bedside Teachings and Writings.* New York: Henry Schuman, Inc. (*n.b.* numerical references to Bean in footnotes refer to aphorisms, not pages.)

Beauchamp TL, Childress JF (2012). *Principles of Biomedical Ethics.* 7th edition, New York: Oxford University Press.

Best JA (2016). The things we have lost. *JAMA* 316; 18:1871.

Bliss M. (1999). *William Osler: A Life in Medicine.* New York: Oxford University Press. This is a comprehensive, one-volume biography.

Bok D (1993). *The Cost of Talent: How Executives and Professionals are Paid and How it Affects America.* New York: The Free Press; 230.

Boutwell B (2014). *John P. McGovern, MD: A Lifetime of Stories.* College Station, TX: Tx A&M U. Press.

Brand P, Yancey, P. (1987). *Fearfully and Wonderfully Made.* Grand Rapids: Zondervan.

Brieger GH (1991). The Fielding H. Garrison Lecture. Classics and character: Medicine and gentility. *Bull Hist Med* 65: 88-109.

Brooks D (2016). The power of altruism. *New York Times*, 8 July 2016.

Brotherton S, Kao A, Crigger BJ (2016) Professing the values of medicine: the modernized AMA code of medical ethics. *JAMA* 316: 1041-2.

Browne, T (1862). *Sir Thomas Browne's Religio Medici, Letter to a Friend Etc., and Christian Morals*. London: Macmillan and Co. Ltd (1926 ed W.A. Greenhill).

Bryan CS (2000). Osler's choice: One person's perspective on the past and future of internal medicine. *Trans Am Clin Climatol Assoc* 111: 164-87.

Bryan CS (2003). Theodore E. Woodward Award. HIV/AIDS, ethics, and medical professionalism: Where went the debate? *Trans Am Clin Climatol Assoc* 114: 353-67.

Bryan CS (1997). *Osler: Inspirations from a Great Physician*. New York: Oxford University Press. An excellent presentation of Osler's ideals.

Bryan CS (1999). L'envoi revisited: The ideal of idealism. *Pharos* 62 (2): 27-31.

Bryan CS (2015). Osler redux: The American College of Physicians at 100. *Lancet* 385: 1720-1.

Bryan CS, Babalay AM (2009). Building character: A model for reflective practice. *Acad Med* 84: 1283-8.

Byrd R (1938). *Alone: The classic story of his greatest adventure.* (Republished by Island Press in 2003.)

Byyny RL, Papadakis MA, Paauw DS, eds. (2015). *Medical Professionalism: Best Practices.* Menlo Park, California: Alpha Omega Alpha Honor Medical Society.

Charon R, Hermann N (2012). A sense of story, or why teach reflective writing? *Acad Med* 87: 5-7.

Cone C (1926). Making ward-rounds with "Dr. Osler." In *Abbott* (1926): 320.

Conti B (2008). *Religio Medici's* profession of faith. Chapter 7 in: Barbour R, Preston C, eds. *Sir Thomas Browne: The World Proposed.* Oxford (UK): Oxford University Press.

Cope Z (1947). *The Diagnosis of the Acute Abdomen in Rhyme*. Oxford: Oxford Medical Publications.

Cope Z (1921). *Early diagnosis of the acute abdomen.* See Silen W (2005).

Coulehan J (2016). What's in your library? "The Leaven of the Humanities" *JAMA* 316: 1340-41.

Coulehan J, Granek IA (2012). "I hope I'll continue to grow": Rubrics and reflective writing in medical education. *Acad Med* 87: 8-10.

Cousins N (1989). *Head First: The Biology of Hope.* New York: E. P. Dutton.

Cousins N, Ed (1982). *The Physician in Literature.* Philadelphia: the Saunders Press.

Covey S (1989). *The Seven Habits of Highly Effective People.* New York: The Free Press.

Cox J (2005). A life in psychiatry and literature: An interview with Robert Coles. *Christianity and Literature* 54:563-75.

Cushing H (1925). *Cushing H. The Life of Sir William Osler.* Oxford: Clarendon Press (two volumes).

Decety J, Yang C, Chen Y (2010). Physicians down-regulate their pain empathy response: An event-related brain potential study. *Neuroimage* 50: 1676-82.

Emanuel E (2016). Attitudes and practices of euthanasia and assisted suicide in the U.S., Canada and Europe. *JAMA* 316: 79-90.

Fins JJ (2015). The expert generalist: A contradiction whose time has come. *Acad Med* 90: 101-14.

Fitzgerald FT (1999). Curiosity. *Ann Intern Med* 130: 70-2.

Frankl V (1986). *Man's search for meaning.* Boston: Beacon Press.

Freeman BS (2013). *The Ultimate Guide to Choosing a Medical Specialty.* Third edition, New York: McGraw-Hill Education/Medical.

Friedson E (2001) *Professionalism: The Third Logic.* Chicago: U of C Press.

Fulton JF (1949). William Osler, the humanist. *Arch Intern Med* 84: 149-58.

Fye WB (1989). William Osler's departure from North America. The price of success. *N Engl J Med* 320 (21): 1425-31.

Gardner AD (1969). Some recollections of Sir William Osler at Oxford. *JAMA* 210: 2265-7.

Ginsburg RB (2016). *My Own Words.* New York: Simon & Schuster.

Golden RL (2015). Paul Revere Osler: The other child. *Proc* (Bay Univ Med Cent) 28: 21-3.

Gourevitch D (1999). The history of medical teaching. *Lancet* 354 Suppl: SIV 33.

Grassi C, Fripp V, Pories S (2016). ACS WiSC addresses ongoing challenges for women in surgery. *ACS Bulletin* 101: 29-33.

Greiner R (2016). 1909: The introduction of the word 'empathy' into English. In: *BRANCH: Britain, Representation and Nineteenth-Century History, Extension of Romanticism and Victorianism on the Net,* Felluga DF, ed. Http://www. branchcollective.org, accessed 23 January 2016.

Groopman J (2007). *How Doctors think.* New York: Houghton Mifflin Company.

Gruen RL, Campbell EG, Blumenthal D (2006). Public roles of US physicians: Community participation, political involvement, and collective advocacy. *JAMA* 296: 2467-75.

Harrell GT (1985). Osler's professorships and his families. *Perspect Biol Med* 29: 77-87.

Harrison TR, Beeson PB, Thorn GW, Resnik WH, Wintrobe HM eds. (1950). *Approach to the patient (Introduction). Principles of Internal Medicine.* New York, NY: McGraw-Hill Book Company; 1-5.

Hinohara S, Niki H, eds. (2001). *Osler's "A Way of Life" and Other Addresses, with Commentary and Annotations.* Durham (NC): Duke University Press.

Hirschtick RE (2016). The quick physical exam. *JAMA* 316: 1363-4.

Holman E (1969). Sir William Osler: Teacher and Bibliophile. *JAMA* 210: 2223-5.

Holmes OW (1892). The young practitioner. In: *The Works of Oliver Wendell Holmes: Medical Essays, 1842-1882.* Standard library edition, volume IX. Boston: Houghton, Mifflin and Company; 370-95.

Inlow WP (1964). The medical man as philosopher: An examination of the pragmatism of William Osler. *Bull Hist Med* 38: 199-225.

JAMA [Eds] (2011). *Care at the Close of Life: Evidence and Experience.* New York: McGraw Hill Medical.

Johnson WB, Ridley CR (2004). *The Elements of Mentoring.* New York: Palgrave Macmillan.

Kaatz A, Carnes M (2014). Stuck in the out group: Jennifer can't grow up, Jane's invisible, and Janet's over the hill. *J Women's Health* (Lchmt) 23: 481-4.

Kahn MW (2008). Etiquette-based medicine. *N Engl J Med* 358: 1988-9.

Kempainen RR, Bartels DM, Veatch PM (2007). Life on the receiving end: A qualitative analysis of health providers' illness narratives. *Acad Med* 82: 207-13.

Kelly, TR. (1992). *A Testament of Devotion.* New York: Harper One.

Kenny NP (2010). Selling our Souls: The Commercialization of Medicine and Commodification of Care as Challenges to Professionalism. The 25th John P. McGovern Ward Lecture, delivered April 27, 2010, at the 40th Meeting of the American Osler Society. American Osler Society: Privately printed (available on the Internet).

Keynes GL, ed. (1951). *Selected Writings of Sir William Osler.* London: Oxford University Press.

Kolata G (2015). *The New York Times Book of Medicine.* New York: Sterling Press.

Krause EA (1996). *Death of the Guilds: Professions, States, and the Advance of Capitalism, 1930 to the Present.* New Haven (CT): Yale University Press.

LaCombe MA, Elpern DJ Eds (2010). *Osler's Bedside Library: Great Writers Who Inspired a Great Physician.* Philadelphia: ACP Press.

Lantos J (1997). *Do We Still Need Doctors?* New York: Routledge.

Leon, PW (1995). *Walt Whitman & Sir William Osler: A Poet and His Physician.* Toronto: ECW Press.

Leykum LK, Lanham HJ, Pugh JA, et al (2014). Manifestations and implications of uncertainty for improving healthcare systems: An analysis of observational and intervention studies grounded in complexity science. *Implement Sci* 9: 165.

Liveanu A (2009). A McGill update of Osler's bedside books list. *McGill J Med* 12: 92-93.

Lown B (1996). *The Lost Art of Healing.* Boston: Houghton, Mifflin & Co.

Lown B (1983). Introduction. In *Cousins N The Healing Heart.* New York W. W. Norton & Co.

Ludmerer KM (2015). *Let Me Heal: The Opportunity to Preserve Excellence in American Medicine.* Oxford: Oxford University Press.

McGovern JP, Burns CR, eds. (1973). *Humanism in Medicine.* Springfield, Illinois: Charles C. Thomas, Publisher.

Maslow AH (1970). *Motivation and Personality.* Second edition, New York: Harper and Row.

Medical professionalism in the new millennium: A physician charter (2002). *Ann Intern Med* 136: 243-6.

Mizrahi T (1986). *Getting Rid of Patients: Contradictions in the Socialization of Physicians.* Brunswick, NJ: Rutgers University Press.

MKR (2016) Do the kind thing and do it first. *Canadian Journal of General Internal Medicine* 11: 6. (MKR are the editor's initials.)

Mullan PC, Kessler DO, Cheng A (2014). Educational opportunities with postevent debriefing. *JAMA* 312: 2333-34.

Murray TJ (2009). Read any good books lately? *McGill J Med* 12: 90-91.

Nation EF (1969). Osler's Alter Ego. *Chest* 56: 531-37.

Nuland S (1988). *Doctors: the biography of medicine.* NY: A.A. Knopf.

O'Conner F (1970). The nature and aim of fiction. In *O'Conner F. Mystery and Manners: Occasional Prose, selected and edited by Sally and Robert Fitzgerald.* New York: Farrar, Straus & Giroux; 86.

Osler W (1937). *A Way of Life.* New York: Paul B. Hoeber, Inc.

Osler W (1899). Address to the students of the Albany Medical College. *Albany Med Ann*; 20: 307-9.

Osler W (1908). *An Alabama Student.* London: Oxford U. Press, 108-58.

Osler W (1932). *Aequanimitas With other Addresses to Medical Students, Nurses, and Practitioners in Medicine* (3rd edition). New York: McGraw-Hill.   (Indented below in alphabetical order are Osler's essays cited in the footnotes by title only, and the page number they appear in that volume.)
Osler W. Aequanimitas, 3.

Osler W. After twenty-five years, 189.

Osler W. Bedside library for medical students, 452.

Osler W. Books and men, 207.

Osler W. Chauvinism in medicine, 263.

Osler W. Doctor and nurse, 13.

Osler W. L'Envoi, 445.

Osler W. Medicine in the nineteenth century, 217.

Osler W. On the educational value of the medical Society, 327.

Osler W. Physic and physicians as depicted in Plato, 45.

Osler W. Teacher and student, 21.

Osler W. Teaching and thinking, 115.

Osler W. The student life, 425.

Osler W. The hospital as a college, 311.

Osler W. The master-word in medicine, 347.

Osler W. The student life, 395.

Osler W. Unity, peace and concord, 425.

Osler W (1908). Elisha Bartlett: A Rhode Island Philosopher. In Osler W, *An Alabama Student*, 108-58.

Osler W (1877). *Introductory lecture on the opening of the forty-fifth session of the medical faculty,* McGill University. Montreal: Dawson Brothers.

Osler W (1897). *Lectures on Angina Pectoris and Allied States.* New York: D. Appleton and Company.

Osler W (1903). On the need of a radical reform in our methods of teaching senior students. *Medical News* [New York] 82: 49-53.

Osler W (1891). On the opening of the Johns Hopkins Medical School to Women [open letters]. In: *Century Mag* 41: 632-7.

Osler W (1899). On the study of pneumonia. *St. Paul Med J.* 1: 5-9.

Osler W (1904). *Science and Immortality.* Boston: Houghton, Mifflin & Co.

Osler W. (1908). Sir Thomas Browne. In Osler W, *An Alabama Student*, 248-77.

Osler W (1910). The faith that heals. *Brit Med J* 2: 1470-2.

Osler W (1907b). The reserves of life. *St. Mary's Hospital Gazette* 13: 95-8.

Osler W (1921). *The Evolution of Modern Medicine*. New Haven: Yale University Press.

Osler W (1897). The function of a state faculty. *Maryland Med J* 37: 73.

Osler W (1885-86). The growth of a profession. *Can Med Surg J* 1885-86; 14: 129-55.

Osler W (1909). The medical library in post-graduate work. *Brit Med J* 2: 925-8.

Osler W (1892). *The Principles and Practice of Medicine*. New York: D. Appleton and Company.

Osler W (1885). Unpublished draft of an address to medical students at the University of Pennsylvania. Montreal: Osler Library of the History of Medicine.

Osler W (1874-75). Valedictory address to the graduates in medicine and surgery, McGill University. *Can Med Surg J* 3: 433-42.

Peabody FW (1927). The care of the patient. *JAMA* 88: 877-82.

Pellegrino ED, Thomasma DC (1993). *The Virtues in Medical Practice*. New York: Oxford University Press.

Penfield W (1949). Neurology in Canada and the Osler centennial. *Can Med Assoc J* 61: 69-73.

Pepper W (1885-6). *A System of Practical Medicine by American Authors*. Philadelphia: Lea Brothers & Co.

Pepper W (1891). Opening address. *Trans Assoc Am Physicians* 6: xv-xx.

Peterson C, Seligman MEP (2004). *Character Strengths and Virtues: A Handbook and Classification*. Washington, DC: American Psychological Association.

Pieper J (1966). *The Four Cardinal Virtues.* Notre Dame: Indiana: University of Notre Dame Press [orig., 1954].

Pieper J (1997). *Faith, Hope, Love.* San Francisco: Ignatius Press [orig., 1962].

Pololi LH et al (2013). Experiencing the culture of academic medicine: gender matters, a national study. *J Gen Int Med* 28: 201-7.

Poses RM, Smith WR (2016). How employed physicians' contracts may threaten their patients and professionalism. *Ann Intern Med* 165: 55-6.

Pratt JH (1920). Osler as his students knew him. *Boston Med Surg J* 182: 338-41.

Pratt JH (1949). Aequanimitas. *Arch Intern Med* 84: 86-92.

Rabinowitz I, Luzzati R, Tamir A, Reis S (2004). Length of patient's monologue, rate of completion, and relation to other components of the clinical encounter: Observational interventional study in primary care. *Brit Med J* 328: 501.

Redelmeier DA (2005). The cognitive psychology of missed diagnoses. *Ann Intern Med* 142: 115-20.

Reiser SJ (2009). *Technological Medicine: The Changing World of Doctors and Patients.* New York: Cambridge University Press.

Roland CG (1982). *Sir William Osler, 1849-1919.* Toronto: The Hannah Institute for the History of Medicine.

Rosenberg CE (1987). *The Cure of Strangers: The Rise of America's Hospital System.*

Schweitzer A (1935). The meaning of ideals in life. (Found on internet at http://myhome.spu.edu/sperisho/ SchweitzerInTheSilcoatian.pdf)

Silen W (2005). *Cope's Early diagnosis of the acute abdomen 21st ed.* NY: Oxford U. Press.

Silverman B, Adler S (2014). *Your Doctors' Manners Matter: Better Health through Civility in the Doctor's Office and in the Hospital.* Alpharetta, GA: Booklogix.

Silverman ME, Murray TJ, Bryan CS (2003). *The Quotable Osler.* Philadelphia: American College of Physicians.

Simpkin AL, Schwartzstein RM (2016). Tolerating uncertainty—the next medical revolution? *NEJM* 375; 18: 1713-15.

Spiro HM (1998). *The Power of Hope: A Doctor's Perspective.* New Haven: Yale U. Press

Starr P (1982). *The Social Transformation of American Medicine.* New York: Basic Books, Inc.

Stevens R (2001). Public roles for the medical profession in the United States: Beyond theories of rise and fall. *Milbank Quarterly* 79: 327-53.

Strauss (1968). *Familiar Medical Quotations.* Boston: Little, Brown and Co.

Thayer WS (1931). *Osler and Other Papers.* Freeport, New York: Books for Libraries Press [republished in 1969].

Thayer WS (1931). Osler the teacher. In Thayer WS. *Osler and Other Papers*; 1-5.

Tumulty PA (1973). *The Effective Clinician: His Methods and Approach to Diagnosis and Care.* Philadelphia: W. B. Saunders.

Vaillant GE (2008). *Spiritual Evolution: A Scientific Defense of Faith.* New York: Broadway Books.

Vallery-Radot R. (1924). *The Life of Pasteur.* NY: Garden City.

VanderVeer J (2014). Anton Chekhov. In Cooper DC ed. *Doctors of Another Calling: Physicians who Are Known Best in Fields Other than Medicine.* Newark: University of Delaware Press.

VanderVeer J (2016). Ambroise Paré *The Oslerian* [newsletter of the American Osler Society] 17(2): 1-3.

VanderVeer J (1999). Euthanasia in the Netherlands. *J Am Coll Surg* 188: 532-37.

VanderVeer J (2012). Let us collaborate with clergy. *Proc* (Bayl Univ Med Cent) 23: 1-3.

Verney RE (1957). *The Student Life: The Philosophy of Sir William Osler.* Edinburgh: E. & S. Livingstone Ltd.

Wald HS, Borkan JM, Taylor JS, et al (2012). Fostering and evaluating reflective practice in medical education. Developing the REFLECT rubric for assessing reflective writing. *Acad Med* 87: 41-50.

Walton DN (1986). *Courage: A Philosophical Investigation.* Berkeley: University of California Press.

Whitehorn J (1963). Education for uncertainty. *Perspect Biol Med* 7: 118-23.

Williams WC (1967). *The Autobiography of William Carlos Williams.* NY: New Directions Press.

Wood LC (2004). *The life and legacy of Francis C. Wood, M.D.* (privately printed).

INTERNET SOURCES CITED:

http://montrealgazette.com/news/local-news/quebec-to-do-away-with-annual-health-checkups (re: Annual physical exams)

www.ncbi.nlm.nih.gov/pubmed/1206 (re: Professionalism)

http://www.my-personality-test.com/personality-type.

http://www.nejm.org/doi/full/10.1056/NEJMicm040708#t=article (re: Sister Mary Joseph Nodule)

http://emedicine.medscape.com/article/775407-clinical (re: thrombosed hemorrhoid)

www.bloomberg.com/news/articles/1993-06-27/governor-caseys-timely- transplant

https://en.wikipedia.org/wiki/Terri_Schiavo_case

https://www.poetryfoundation.org/poems-and-poets/poems/
    detail/44433
http://myhome.spu.edu/sperisho/SchweitzerInTheSilcoatian.pdf
    (Schweitzer on happiness)
https://www.aamc.org/cim/ (AAMC Careers in Medicine)
https://news.aamc.org/medical-education/article/women-
    enrolling-medical-school-10-year-high/ (AAMC Video on
    Diversity)

SUPPLEMENTAL WORTHY REFERENCES
(See also Bedside Library recommendations.)

Baltasar Gracián (1647) *The Art of Worldly Wisdom.* (Tr.
    Maurer) Published by Doubleday © 1992. This Spanish
    Jesuit priest's 300 pithy paragraphs combine a virtuous
    approach to life with a sly success philosophy.
Berlinger N (2005) *After Harm: Medical Error and the Ethics
    of Forgiveness.* Baltimore: Johns Hopkins University Press.
    A good read about how to deal with medical mistakes.
Davenport W ed. (1962) *The Good Physician: A Treasury of
    Medicine.* New York: Macmillan & Company. An excellent
    compendium of works by and about physicians through the
    ages.
Epictetus (~100 CE) *The Art of Living: The Classical Manual
    on Virtue, Happiness, and Effectiveness.* San Francisco:
    Harper Collins © 1995. In an early section of this manual
    for Roman Soldiers, you will recognize that theologian
    Reinhold Niebuhr's "Serenity Prayer" is based on Epictetus.
Humphrey HJ (2010). *Mentoring and Fostering Professionalism
    in Medical Education.* Philadelphia: American College of
    Physicians.

Lo B (2013). *Resolving Ethical Dilemmas: A Guide for Clinicians. 5ᵗʰ ed.* Philadelphia: Williams & Wilkins. (Using a case-by-case approach, Lo, an internist and ethicist at UCSF, deals with ethical dilemmas commonly encountered in clinical medicine.)

MacLeod R (2001). Learning from Sir William Osler about the teaching of palliative care. *Journal of Palliative Care* 17: 265-9.

Medical professionalism in the new millennium: A physician charter (2002). *Ann Intern Med* 136: 243-6.

Paul O (1991). *The Caring Physician: The Life of Dr. Francis W. Peabody.* Boston: The Francis A. Countway Library of Medicine.

Reid EG (1931).*The Great Physician: A Short Life of Sir William Osler.* NY: Oxford U. Press. A biography of Osler, more informal and shorter than Cushing (1925) or Bliss (1999), but not so well documented.

Seneca (~40 CE). *On the Shortness of Life.* (Tr. Costa) Penguin version © 1997. Seneca, the Stoic philosopher promotes the value of a quiet mind, helpful advice in the hectic modern world.

MY NOTES

MY NOTES

MY NOTES

MY NOTES

MY NOTES

MY NOTES

MY NOTES